With D'Annunzio in Fiume

WITH D'ANNUNZIO
IN FIUME

WITH THE ADDITION OF *WE ARDITI*,
AN ESSAY ON ITALY'S ELITE SHOCK TROOPS OF THE FIRST WORLD WAR

— BY MARIO CARLI —

TRANSLATED BY CIARÁN Ó LAIGHLÉIS

ANTELOPE HILL PUBLISHING

CONTENTS

With D'Annunzio in Fiume

We Arditi

PROLOGUE:
HOW I GOT TO FIUME

Adventures of a Soldier in the
First Year of the Armistice

My adventures of a political and disciplinary nature, or more precisely, the Italian General Staff's persecution of me, had their origins in March 1919. After my manifesto for the Arditi Association had fallen under the eyes of the capital's command superiors, an investigation was ordered. I was interrogated, examined, and probed to the point of exhaustion. The Division Command, Army Corps, and the War Ministry made it their duty to waste massive amounts of my most useful free time, subjecting me to interminable interrogations, cretinous questionnaires, and lectures stuffed with rhetoric, which were repeated again and again until I regurgitated everything the regulation says—page x, paragraph y, directive n—about the soldier's duty to avoid politics, founding associations, abusing the press, and so on and so forth.

The conclusion of this intricate drudgery of martial bureaucracy was a ten-day close arrest for having issued an appeal to the

Arditi, inviting them to form an association, before requesting the authorization of the higher authorities.

My arrest was ordered in the name of the war minister, General Caviglia. But I have good reason to believe that he knew nothing, or, at the very least, was forced to allow a measure taken by the overzealous middle command. The fact is, the same day the penalty was communicated to me, I was paid a visit at our association headquarters by Caviglia's personal secretary, Captain Rotigliano. He had come to tell me that the minister deplored the measure he was *forced* to take against me, and that, when my punishment was complete, he would like to see me at the Ministry.

And so I went. In the flesh, the victor of Vittorio Veneto smiled and repeatedly expressed his sympathy, inviting me to take things with resigned patience. He made the best of impressions on me. He seemed a man of the new Italy: a true soldier, a fort of a man. He approved the creation of the Arditi Association, and even suggested how it should be formed.

He assured me that my activities would not be sabotaged by the superiors, especially given how ably I had avoided the rigors of the disciplinary regulation.

Grumbling about the untimely dissolution (Zuppelli's masterpiece![1]) of the Arditi Corps, he said something that endeared me to him immediately:

"Ah, I wouldn't want to see them here, the Arditi!"

"Where, then?" I asked.

"In Split."

"Excellency," I said at once, "just say the word, and we'll all head to Dalmatia."

He smiled. He saw the Arditi Futurist in me, for whom

---

[1] Vittorio Italico Zuppelli, an Italian general who preceded Caviglia as Minister of War.

conceiving a plan and executing that plan are one and the same thing. He gave my hand a hearty shake, professing the utmost admiration for the Arditi in general, and the Futurists in particular.

"In my army corps I had an assault unit, which I handled like a man handles his woman: jealously. And everyone wanted to take them away from me!"

×   ×   ×

A few days later, the veterans' celebration took place in Rome. It was a wretched event, left to the last minute, without the slightest sincerity or warmth, with the infantry brigades reaching Rome by night, seen by no one, like a band of thieves. That day a cavalry regiment arrived, and it was only natural that Mayor Colonna, a former cavalryman himself, would be more moved by this than by the arrival of the infantry worn out by victory.

An official reception was solemnly decreed. To avoid displaying any clear bias, every division was invited. Only the Arditi were excluded, with the justification being that they did not constitute an organic unit in Rome, but were rather the debris of various other units, spread across the infantry depots.

Made aware of this odious injustice against the Arditi, I acted to right it, protesting at the headquarters, writing in the papers, and telephoning the minister's cabinet—all in vain.

Everyone declared themselves unconditional admirers of the Arditi, but no one wanted to *assume* (listen! listen!) *the tremendous responsibility* of inviting them to the ceremony. Only at the last minute, a phonogram from the division authorized me to have them *attend* the troop parade, in the box assigned to . . . the Garibaldian veterans!

Around two hundred gathered at San Carlo al Corso, in front of the Association. We filed out along the streets of Rome, with our tattered pennant, singing "Giovinezza!"[2] and receiving enthusiastic support from the public, who understood our protest.

I then led them near the Colosseum to drink a fojetta.[3] As we passed the Capitoline Hill, I was invited to speak. I avoided launching an attack on the parade organizers. I simply said that we, who had fought for the greatness of Italy, and only for that, had no need for the flowers or applause lavished by those who represented a treacherous and pompous domestic front.

These words, addressed to the character of my listeners, and more disdainful than subversive, were recorded by one of the very few bourgeois present (without doubt a spy for the police), and arrived almost immediately in the Via della Pilotta offices. After a few days another ten-day close arrest order came in a yellow envelope, "for having given a speech to the Arditi, inciting them, etc. etc."

×   ×   ×

Toward the end of April, I had the pride and honor of helping revive the delirious "radiant May" atmosphere in Rome.[4] Almost every day, even twice a day, we called on Romans to gather in the streets, electrified them with violent discourse, made them speak as one for our Fiume and Dalmatia, against the Paris decisions. When the two "elders," who for an instant became capable of Italian pride, abandoned the Conference and came to Rome,[5] the people were so whipped up in their favor that I don't believe I've ever

---

[2] Italian for "youth." This song was popular among Italian soldiers during World War I, and became known as the "Hymn of the Arditi." It was the official hymn of the Italian Fascist Party and army.

[3] A white wine from Lazio.

[4] "Maggio radioso," a period of popular, patriotic demonstrations throughout Italy in 1915 demanding the country enter WWI. D'Annunzio delivered a famous speech on May 12th asking Italians to throw all traitors into the sewers.

[5] The Paris Peace Conference.

seen such a frenzy, such a compact of spirits. The arrival of Orlando at Rome station had the imprint of delirious triumph: it was the free will of a people, expressing itself at a dramatic hour, despite all the diplomatic oppression and international fear.[6] In front of the station there were around two thousand officials, and there was the whole people, men and women. There were the wounded, and finally, there were all the Arditi of Rome. I wanted them to pull Orlando's car on ropes all the way to the Quirinal. It wasn't intended as an act of servility, but rather an act in perfect key with the universal state of mind. The Arditi would triumphantly lead him who had managed to encapsulate the boldest tendency of the national soul with the cry: "Italy knows the ways of hunger, not those of dishonor!"[7]

How wonderfully these divine words resounded, and (alas) how immediate their refutation was upon contact with the vile parliamentary air, always ready for dishonorable dealings!

This atmosphere of idealism steadily sputtered out, through the direct action of the government under the ratchet of Montecitorio,[8] but also due to us, wanting at all costs to keep that atmosphere alive, until we looked like dangerous fanatics. The leaders were all quarantined: in Naples, Luigi Granturco got a fortress arrest; in Rome, Michelangelo Zimolo was locked in a fort; and I was removed from Rome as fast as possible.

On the evening of April 27th, I received a note from the division command, inviting me to visit the Celio Military Hospital the next morning and submit to a checkup. I smelled danger, knowing parliament was opening that day, and protests were expected. But I went all the same. I was also called up by the police

---

[6] Vittorio Emanuele Orlando, Italian Prime Minister from October 1917 to June 1919. The other "elder" was Sidney Sonnino, Orlando's foreign minister.

[7] "Boldest" is given as "*la più ardita.*"

[8] The lower house of the Italian parliament.

commissioner, who wanted to personally entreat me to avoid any public protest that might aim to coerce the will of the parliament. I gave no such commitment; I simply said that I had no intention of organizing anything, but that I was convinced that the protest would form automatically.

Then I proceeded to Celio, knowing they had a trap for me. After the adjutant asked me to wait, an infantry major arrived with an order from the division, asking me to quickly prepare my things and leave with him on the first train for the Cremona depot.

Indignant, I protested against being policed out of the capital, escorted and guarded like a common crook, and because my official recovery period had not yet come to an end, and no regulation gave superiors the liberty to exact this double abuse of power. The major shrugged his shoulders, insisting that he was merely executing orders. So I started following him, after a futile attempt to telephone general Caviglia's cabinet.

I dragged the poor man all over Rome as he played policeman. I don't know which of us was the more sequestered.

At the Arditi Association there was a wave of indignation at the news of my forced departure. Some tried setting things in motion for me, including Giuriati and Ratti,[9] who in the end couldn't prevent my departure, given the harsh climate. Later, it became even more difficult.

At the station we met another division official who came to announce that the major was relieved from departing with me, and that I was welcome to defer my departure to the following evening. When the gentlemen suddenly realized their gaffe and tried to fix it, I simply thanked them for their generosity and departed all the same.

I left with two great and legitimate satisfactions: 1) having

---

[9] Giovanni Giuriati was an Italian fascist who collaborated with D'Annunzio.

launched from Trajan's column the first invitation urging Italians to join the list of volunteers for Fiume and Dalmatia. In this I was a pioneer, and received more than three hundred signatures on the first day; 2) having the Arditi pennant waved from the Quirinal balcony by an adjutant and magnificent fighter from the Battle of Damiani.[10]

Speaking of the Quirinal, I must describe precisely a certain incident, which could potentially lead to misunderstanding or tendentious interpretations.

The day of Orlando's arrival from Paris, I reached the gate of the Royal Palace at the front of the demonstration. I was all set to leave, when an Ardito came and brought me a package of manifestos, printed that morning, bearing my appeal for volunteers. As they were being distributed through the crowd, I had the idea of giving one to General Diaz, since he had shown support for the initiative.

I headed toward the palace entrance, where the cars were just arriving. The general had already passed through, and the attendant at the door offered to announce my arrival.

Indeed, this zealous functionary went right in and announced me. A few minutes later the palace majordomo came to inform me that *His Majesty* was waiting for me.

"But there must be a misunderstanding," I protested. "I never requested to speak with the king, only with General Diaz."

"You will find him upstairs," replied the bearded, liveried majordomo. "In any case you have been announced, and His Majesty awaits you in the salon."

It was impossible to sneak off. He accompanied me to the steps, as my name rang out repeatedly, as if it were that of Napoleon.

---

[10] The Quirinal Hill is one of the Seven Hills of Rome.

"Captain Carli . . . ! It's Captain Carli . . . ! Captain Carli is here!"

It was like some grotesque operetta: a Futurist in the Royal Palace! Announced in such a manner! I knew it was worth the effort, since I'd have a story to tell my friends. Indeed, Bruno Corra and Settimelli,[11] passionate hunters of bizarre comedy, were highly amused.

I remember precisely all the details of the scene. Hardly had I set foot in the hall, when a general ran to meet me, saying:

"You're captain Carli? Come, come: His Majesty is waiting."

The king was in fact in the middle of the room, surrounded by other generals.

He took my hand, spoke warmly, sympathetically, questioning me with curiosity. He gave me the impression of a simple man, without pretension or ceremony, absolutely common, almost inept, almost timid.

I believe I never observed the rules of conduct, because I don't recall having called him "Sire" at any point, and didn't wait to be asked a question before talking. I don't know if I seemed like an uneducated man, or inattentive; he certainly felt that I brought a breath of fresh air, the popular spirit, to the closed and severe Palace. It was the heart of fighting Italy that he heard speaking, to the heart of the man called—with atrocious irony—the first soldier of Italy.

This is why, swayed by first impressions, there remains in me at least a stroke of almost painful good feeling for a man who will have to *fatefully* renounce, will have to cede, to the beating tide of new times, while bearing upon his conscience far fewer offenses and far fewer errors than all of his ministers.

---

[11] Bruno Corra is the pseudonym of Bruno Ginanni Corradini, who, along with Carli and Emilio Settimelli, founded the Futurist magazines *Il Centauro* and *La Rivista*. Settimelli and Carli also started the newspaper *L'Impero*.

In Exile

So I headed to Cremona, confident that soon a ministerial order would recall me from my exile.

In the days that followed, the Roman *Popolo d'Italia* correspondent sent the following note to his paper, which was reproduced with a sympathetic comment in the *Ardito*:

How We Are Rewarded

The captain of the Arditi, Mario Carli, president of the Roman Fascio di Combattimento,[12] was forced to return to his depot days before his leave had expired, for having taken part in a patriotic demonstration.

The measure was arbitrary and unjust, because Captain Carli, while he did take part in patriotic demonstrations for Dalmatia and Fiume (which he considers an honor), also made sure to prevent demonstrators from becoming impulsive and engaging in hostilities in front of particular embassies.

The actions of Captain Carli, demonstrating good sense and responsibility, were documented in the firsthand report of our paper, and others in the capital.

We ask Minister Caviglio if it is just to respond to merit with punishment, or if, inspired by his most noble sentiments, he would instead consider redress for our comrade in arms.

The Offense Against Holy Discipline

On May 18th, in the second issue of *Ardito*, I published what became "that notorious incriminating article," which made more

---

[12] A fascio is a branch of an Italian fascist political organization.

noise than all of my books.

It was this article that caused the war minister to issue a circular telegram banning the sale and reading in barracks of the Bolshevik journal *L'Ardito*, for standing against discipline, the institutions, etc., etc.

Reading is believing:

Arditi, Not Gendarmes

With his most recent circular, the war minister has ordered the restoration of the assault units.

This is nothing to be happy about.

The measure, about which the least possible amount of noise has been made, comes too late, at an inappropriate moment. Apart from the fact the Arditi have not been reunited with their old units, such a measure aims, as the circular confirms, to use, according to their special, characteristic forms, the Arditi Corps in the *services* for which the troops are currently employed.

What are these "services"?

Guarding barracks, forts, and powder kegs? I don't think so. What *special* part could the Arditi possibly play in these utterly common functions of lowly militia? None.

Perhaps it is something to do with public order? Cordons, patrols, armed sentries in various cities more or less shaken by Bolshevik mines? We have reason to believe that this is the correct hypothesis.

So, in that case, dear Minister, your decision not only fails to raise our spirits, but in fact deeply hurts us.

×   ×   ×

You who claim to *know* and *love* the Arditi (to *know* us is pre-cisely to *love* us) are now inflicting the worst of humiliations, turn-ing them into cops and government goons, believing you under-stand their deepest ambitions: that of witnessing the restoration of those beautiful assault battalions.

No, Your Excellency, it is too late for that.

There was no need to disband the battalions.

You didn't have to cede to pressure from the social-*boche*-Gio-littians when they so astutely ordered the disappearance of the sacred flame of Italy, so that dissolvent Leninism might triumph.[13]

Now that you have (finally!) understood our function as regu-lators and precursors of the Futuristic march of our people, now that you have noticed we are capable of thwarting anti-Italian con-spiracies, you grab hold of us and scatter us in random depots, turning us into faithful and obedient praetorian guards.

Once more, you are mistaken. The second error will not fix the first, but will rather aggravate it.

×   ×   ×

With the units disbanded, we managed to locate each and every Ardito, and unite them under new leadership. We provided comfort against national ingratitude, and supported them as they entered other battles.

But if spontaneously, in the name of beauty and poetry with which they vanquished the Austrians, they undertook to wipe the Bolshevik rabble off our streets, they would never have the same ardor or purifying fury were they boxed in and controlled.

They feel tied up, dishonored by a carabiniere varnish that will

---

[13] Giovanni Giolitti, former prime minister, was opposed to Italy joining WWI against former allies Germany and the Austro-Hungarian Empire.

brutally extinguish their divine flames.[14]

We were not developed for such tasks, Your Honor. So leave us as before, dissolved and dismembered. Then we can be more useful to the nation. Because, let it be known, *we are volunteers who want to intervene if and when we want* and in whatever form we please.

Confuse us with cops . . . pfft!

Interrogations, Arrests, and Other Policing

At the same time as the telegraphic order banning the reading of *L'Ardito* to soldiers, there came another telegram from the Genoa Army Corps asking me if I knew who had authored a particular article. I responded that I recognized it and would assume full responsibility. Then I was invited to present myself to the Army Corps headquarters, where I was interrogated.

The interrogation—which I was told was ordered by the Minister—lasted five days. A good old Piedmontese general, extremely erudite when it came to regulations, made me read a mountain of circulars and depositions that apparently demonstrated that, even if I had not committed any actual crime, I had at least committed a great offense against discipline, inciting soldiers to disobedience, speaking with insufficient reverence (or even acknowledging chain of command) to no less than His Excellency the War Minister, and so forth.

I've already expressed in sufficient detail my personal admiration and sympathy for General Caviglia. It's only logical then that the polemic energy of my article was addressed more to the government body, the ministerial organ that produces all these circulars, than to the minister himself, who always fascinated me as a

---

[14] The carabinieri is the Italian gendarmerie.

true soldier and brilliant man, despite being somewhat bureaucratized by the environment.

When the interrogation was complete I was sent back to my depot, but not before the head of the Army Corps General Staff (I don't know why, but hateful tasks are always assigned to the head of the General Staff) ordered me, on behalf of General Lequio, to suspend any collaboration with *L'Ardito* until the minister had come to a decision.

I left Genoa with a curious memory of each session of questioning, which all took place in a small cold room, alternating with visits to the Futurist exhibition, where Marinetti, Pinna, Depero, Degasperi, Cavagnetto, Guglielmino, Forti, and other Futurists had created incessant fanfares of electric, disorderly, polychromatic noise.

In Cremona, about two months passed without the slightest sign of life from my superiors. The investigation appeared to have been put to sleep, and I was almost certain that Caviglia had goodnaturedly buried it. So I occupied myself with obtaining leave, to which I was entitled due to my volunteer status.

It wasn't easy to convince the depot commandant that my leave was due. A mechanical and monumental process was set in motion to ascertain my rights, and whole weeks passed before I had what I wanted. Everyone was going home (even those more junior than me), the minister recommended prompt demobilization, and the country demanded the involvement of young men in civil life, as I remained rotting away in a depot, useless to the country and to myself, exasperated and eaten away by mounting impatience, incapable of work or activity, inertly and feverishly waiting for a decision that was stuck.

Finally, one morning, the colonel requested that I visit. After I rushed over, it was announced that the long-awaited day of liberation had finally come, and I was shown the already prepared notice of leave, lacking only a signature. I was near mad with joy: freedom! Ah, divine freedom! Finally! Finally I had it in my hands!

As I waited for the required signature, the post arrived.

The adjutant-major opened it, sorted it, and distributed it in silence. Minutes later, the colonel had me come to his office, gave me a slightly mortified look, and handed me a card. I read it. The war minister announced that he had referred me to the disciplinary council, and ordered that my leave be refused, as I waited to be called to Rome. I was stupefied. I'd been plunged once more into the gray torpor of waiting.

Given that the disciplinary council had removed me from service for some months, I decided to take a trip to Milan to get my friends up to speed and put some things in order. Naturally, I didn't ask permission from my colonel, a fearful man incapable of initiative, who would never have given it.

Upon my return, he thought it best to having me locked up in a tiny room, for fear of losing me again. My first five days of real prison were spent with the bugs and mice. The innumerable prior arrests had been passed at home or in a hotel room, where I never wanted for the company of some generous friend, moved by my fate. This time I was placed in the barracks, with all of its spectral horror, its cold squalor, its stink, its gloomy damp, its penetrating melancholy.

This time it was one window with iron bars, isolation, mold, cobwebs, tragic silence, a view of an abandoned vegetable patch and a roof full of countless detritus, the miserable lullaby of the Austrians next door, the skeletal bed of iron creaking like a casket, overrun by battalions of filthy bedbugs—alas, it was the full range of prison horror, all of its dreadful aridity.

On It Goes . . .

After the five days passed, I was called to Rome, where I was interrogated by three solemn, bearded generals, "impassible and impenetrable," and promptly returned to Cremona with no explanation. I expected, as was the general opinion, either demotion for serious offenses against discipline, or at least a few months in a fortress.

But the punishment for my "Prussianly stupid disgrace" was to come in a different form.

With my case lacking sufficient severity for demotion, the disciplinary council held back on immediate judgment. Meanwhile, to prevent me going free, to remove an excessively dynamic and dangerous individual from circulation, a cop-like act of retaliation was contrived against something that had already been punished.

It was a quarrel that took place one June night in Piacenza with a carabiniere sergeant. Abusing his position as protector of public order, he had offended against discipline by failing to observe the respect owed to me as a captain. I was returned to my depot in Cremona for a twenty-day arrest.

I protested in writing, placing responsibility squarely on the sergeant's attitude. Initially they rejected the appeal. Then, after some editing, it was finally received. Fearing perhaps the consequences of political persecution, Minister Albricci couldn't demote me for the article in *L'Ardito*. But he also didn't want to grant me leave, out of fear of immediate reprisals (every tyrant imagines a spirit of vengeance in all those he persecutes, though it doesn't necessarily exist). So he went and dug up the Most Esteemed Sergeant's file and concluded that I had gravely offended a public functionary by wrongfully accusing him. Without the slightest investigation, without interrogating me or examining my testimony, they saddled me with *three months of fortress arrest*, not counting the previous twenty-day arrest.

Thus the Nitti government,[15] loyal to their law-enforcer principles, gave their backing to a pot-bellied draft dodger and most odious tool of the police, the almighty father of blackmail and abuse of power, and ideal servant of his exceedingly reactionary master.

Once again, law enforcement had got one over on a soldier given no chance to defend himself or make a counter-accusation. During this period, for the last time before September 12th, I met Lieutenant Colonel Gabriele D'Annunzio taking a train to Venice to celebrate the anniversary of the flight over Vienna. At the station I exclaimed with regret:

"Oh, how I felt your absence that day when the two elders made their clandestine departure from Paris! You can imagine how I tried to prevent them from leaving, by violence. But we needed you with your Arditi!"

Informed of my disciplinary procedures, he asked:

"What can I do to end this iniquity?"

I reassured him. Demotion didn't scare me. Parting, he saluted me with the words: "See you in the new Italy!"

×　　　×　　　×

So I went straight to prison, the same one in which I had already spent five days. I was once again fighting off bedbugs, mice, cobwebs, and other housemates, who managed to inject me with regretful nostalgia for the accursed trench lice, the glorious torturer of our suffering flesh in the most beautiful and necessary of wars. Oh, how I thought of the trenches in those days! How I

---

[15] Francesco Saverio Nitti was the prime minister of Italy from 1919–1920. He was opposed to fascism in Italy.

would have offered my life once more, and suffered horrible agony each day, for ideals worthy of the ardor and energy that stirred inside me!

Bedbugs rehabilitated the lice, mice made the wharf rats beautiful, the bars on the window made wire fences fascinating.

Compared to the passive nonexistence of prison, trench life was like a lost paradise, of which I was undeserving due to some atrocious crime I'd committed.

In the end, when I wasn't thinking of the absurdity of my situation, and of the supreme good of freedom, I did find strands of humor that provided a good deal of diversion, and only hurt because I had no friends with whom to share them.

You should have seen the ravenous throng that assaulted my white bed in the evening. All it took was to undress under the twenty-five-candela light bulb that blazed like the sun of the future over my bed.[16] From the mattress and every cranny of the metal frame, attracted to the succulent odor of sweaty human summer-evening skin, emerged the ranks that would expropriate my pores, marching with their innumerable arriviste feet over the roller coaster of the bed-sheet until they reached me.

I just let them come, the aggressive little discs. My hairy legs remained immobile like wooded mountain slopes full of mystery and promise. From every corner their gradual, tranquil march continued, encouraged by the electric sun hanging in mid-air, and by the immobility of the landscape exuding the long-awaited promise of an unexplored mine.

Then, when they were just one leap from my body, when they were just about to get their prehensile little proboscises into my flesh, I'd retract my legs with lightning speed, and with the point of my avenging shiv I took their assault formation head on,

---

16 *"Sole dell'avvenire,"* a communist slogan.

turning them into a ruddy blob on the nearly immaculate purity of the sheet.

It was rabid, violent, cackling carnage. You should have seen the speed and accuracy. It was as if I'd done nothing else in life: I was a consummate killer of bugs. At times it was indeed "pointless bloodshed," because no matter how many I killed, even more would appear. It was the inexorable climb of a bloodthirsty proletarian blindly drawn to the red seen through my radioscopic flesh. There was nothing to do but jump from the bed, yank the sheet from the mattress, shake it out the window, and then hermetically seal the mattress with it, and trust in the terrorized imbecility of the survivors.

Keeping guard, my shiv never out of reach, I managed to occasionally get some sleep.

Meanwhile there were people looking out for me. Distant friends remembered me with affection touched by nostalgia, calling for my liberation. Look at these two stupendously fraternal articles, published at the time.

Free Mario Carli! The Inventor of
"A Meditative Smoke over Death"

I first met Mario Carli eleven years ago in Florence. Slender, bespectacled, elegant, he surprised me with some of his artistic leanings, which seemed so out of key with his aristocratic profile. His first words were a real bounty—enough for me to evaluate his character. I introduced myself with the maximum synthesis and the maximum loyalty.[17]

I immediately liked him. I immediately respected him. I

---

[17] *"Sintetismo,"* a term associated with the avant-garde art movements of the time, including Futurism.

immediately chose him as a brother in arms, in beauty, in heroism.

For eleven years we worked elbow to elbow, with Carli constantly revealing new depths of strength, brilliance, and generosity. In our group, he had right from the start a certain *celebrity* for his daring gestures enacted with the most impassible facial expression ever seen. That *resolute* face, alert, the proud mouth and soft, wide eyes behind thick lenses, never faltered for even the most violent emotions. Slaps, blows, insults, protests, reckless leaps, adventures, never caused even the slightest wrinkle of alarm.

Kissed, embraced, and just about suffocated by the Roman crowd in the days of Vittorio Veneto, he remained impassive, with barely a trace of joy on his lips. Raised above all those crazed heads he spoke just a scant few words:

"Romans, we vanquished Austria, but it's not enough! We need to invade Bavaria, to crush Germany!"

The crowd applauded the dignified Ardito in frenzy.

×   ×   ×

Mario Carli was "discharged" from the war due to severe myopia. He didn't stop for a minute. He volunteered and became a second lieutenant. His whole military life was a fight to reach the front. Myopia forced him back. But his stubborn faith allowed him to finally reach it. He was in the trenches for long, harsh months.

Mario Carli probably performed the *strangest patrols* of the war. Many times he had to explore while guided by the hands of his soldiers. Could anyone see anything? He even caught his head in enemy barbed wire.

We laughed at the story. "Nobody but Carli!" He invented the idea of smoking a pipe over Death to help his weak digestion.

×   ×   ×

But there's a more intimate side to his heroism that few are familiar with. Mario Carli's mother had a poor heart and had to preserve herself from all emotion. She was a hot-tempered southerner, passionate, a *mother* in very fiber of her being, the essence of maternity. She was a noble Italian soul with total feeling for the spirit of duty. How could she not suffer, when her son was her whole life?

Carli's volunteering seemed *almost* a form of cruelty toward his mother. His second period of volunteering with the Arditi met with harsh judgment from some of those most devoted to Italy. He had tried to conceal his activities, and for a while he succeeded. Then she discovered his secret. I witnessed (I confess) scenes that tore my virile heart to shreds.

I brought the news of Mario's injury to his mother, tried to console her, and supported her as she faltered and swooned, which could have been fatal.

×   ×   ×

Mario Carli is a restless and exquisite journalist. He published magisterial articles in the *Centauro, La Rivista, L'Ardito, Il Popolo d'Italia,* and *Roma Futurista.* He's the author of the novel *Retroscena,* of *Notti Filtrate, Seduzioni,* and *Addio mia sigaretta.*

He is one of the few who are really noteworthy, and an artist in the deepest sense. He's brilliant, strange, elegant—a modern. His work is part of our artistic heritage. He honors Italy, as do his Ardito-Futurist guts.

×   ×   ×

Upon returning from the front after an injury sustained at So-larolo in a triumphant assault, he fought tirelessly against the enemies of the nation. Rome saw him at the head of every demonstration against anti-Italians and for victory. His articles flashed like his unstoppable dagger against traitors and wimps. Military order thought they could strike him down with three months of fortress arrest.

I will not argue. Discipline is discipline. But here is the truly monstrous thing: the deserters and the lifers are now being amnestied! It is simply not possible that such a monstrous thing could happen in Italy! Mario Carli must be given amnesty and liberated!

He is a great artist, a volunteer, a war casualty, a fantastic fighter, a true hero of military and civil life, an immense, generous, thoroughly elegant Italian soul. Free him!

Liberate this brave soldier, liberate this great poet, give him back to Italy, give him back his noble existence: he is one of the new Italians building the greatest Italy!

Settimelli.

From *The Enemies of Italy*—September 11th

The Mario Carli "Case"

Mario Carli is becoming a "case."

The Mario Carli "case." The consecrated phrase, the seal of public opinion. When a man, in one way or another, comes out of his shell, he is suddenly cataloged in the filing cabinet of public chitchat.

The rigid little functionary, somewhat idiotic but elegant, a little stiff, but upright, who dedicates the maximum mental energy to Albricci's latest circular on uniforms,[18] thinks with a disdainful, bored grimace of the Mario Carli "case."

The pot-bellied, tranquil bourgeois, accustomed to the slow evolution of his sluggish imagination, is unsettled, made weak and foolish, by this terrible infraction of the rules, and of the quiet life: that is the Mario Carli "case."

The reddest of socialist officials, an *Avanti* contributor,[19] and the blackest of Jesuits writing for *L'Unità Cattolica*, slap their bellies in supreme joy, laughing their heads off, thinking of the Mario Carli "case."

Rubbish.

What rubbish, this profound intelligence, from the worm-eaten brain of a minister, horny for authority, spreading through a disciplinary council to grossly obtuse café chatter.

We deny the right of such people to talk of the Mario Carli "case." It is for us, for us soldiers, for us Arditi, for us Futurists.

It has the imprint of our rebellion, the rapid line of our impertinence.

At a time when there is bitter debate between intervention and defeatism, when heroes are slapped in the face and jails are opened, when some idiot deputy asks those *responsible* for the war to defer to the court, this punishment counts as open hostility toward us, free citizens brought to arms, against the will of all, for us, proud people, who topple the wobbly governors and military careerists, we who willed and won the war, in a frenetic impulse of vigorous revolution.

This is an attempt to castrate us, to which we respond with the domineering ostentation of our bronzed virility.

---

[18] Alberico Albricci was an Italian general in World War I.

[19] The official paper of the Italian Socialist Party.

We hurl in your faces these simple words of Mario Carli himself: *"Consider me in the trenches! Long live Italy!"*

×   ×   ×

Simple words, from which reverberate, more vividly than ever, the irrepressible right of the soldier to intervene in the political fortune of the country.

Because this "case," which papers of every stripe are blathering about, comes down to this: a precise and determined will to gag those who fought.

We don't believe the gentlemen who had to read and judge the famous article by Carli were so stupid to really find all the evil there that they claimed. They *had to* arrive at that judgment. The order came from above, cooked up by two ministries, the one for war and the other for internal affairs.

A cop-like maneuver.

Mario Carli committed two grave wrongs against the current holders of government: 1) having called together the Arditi, and having been the creator of that vigilant and ready organization, against which all efforts at defeatism crash to the ground; 2) having organized the first Fasci di Combattimento in Rome, awakening the old city, gutless and marrowless, where it was always so fun to fabricate political schemes.

Terrible wrongs, perilous forms of post-war *intervention*.

In the effort to punish Mario Carli, who was, during the whole winter, the ardent soul of every protest, the most dogged fighter, the most indomitable Ardito, there is an effort to punish a whole *tendency*.

Here is why. The incriminating article was written on May 18th. The first investigation, ordered by Minister Caviglia, concluded on the first of June, resulting in a simple admonition.

Halfway through July the affair was *dug up* almost elegantly, and a second investigation was ordered.

Why? With what right, while the decree granting amnesty to deserters was just being finalized?

×   ×   ×

A declaration of war, then. So be it.

The punishment of the brave and the liberation of the cowardly is a clear declaration of alliance. From this point on, blows against Nitti or Serrati and attacks against the government or defeatism are equivalent terms.[20]

We are happy with this.

The targets are all gathered around a single mass of nameless filth.

We, meanwhile, declare again our indisputable right to play an active role in Italy's political struggle.

Nothing will trip us up.

No obstacle is hard enough to block our path. Our love of our nation has all the infinite momentum of flight.

We will hit our target.

We do not claim this right in the name of sacrifices endured. We are great; we could not care less about recognition. We affirm our *right*, nothing else. *Right*—a tough and cutting word, and Roman, which needs no justification.

We'll discuss this again at the next elections.

Meanwhile, in solidarity with our persecuted friend, as a practical step toward completing our program, we propose the

---

[20] Giacinto Menotti Serrati was an Italian communist and newspaper editor.

candidacy of Mario Carli, Futurist-Ardito of the Fasci di Combattimento.

Giuseppe Bottai.

From *Roma Futurista*—September 14th, 1919.

×   ×   ×

Twelve days had passed, when one morning my orderly had left the *Popolo d'Italia* open enough for me to catch the sensational news: Gabriele D'Annunzio, with Ganatieri and the Arditi, had entered Fiume.

From that moment on, my imprisonment became an intolerable inferno. Up to then I'd been able to handle the corrosive submission of three months of slavery, which would tighten day by day like some gradual torture. Now that *outside* things were happening, now that there was a fight, bringing greatness to Italy and light to the world, I felt in the truest sense like an incarcerated beast.

Now I only thought, lived, or breathed to escape. I occupied myself completely with preparing my departure. Naturally, by will alone, I could have escaped immediately, even though my colonel had his eye on me. But I wanted my escape to reach perfection, and give me a chance to reach Fiume. Leaving prison wasn't really the issue: reaching Fiume was.

The inertia of that period had left vast sums of energy in my nerves that I needed to discharge as soon as possible. In Fiume there were things to get done. Even if I couldn't be among the first there, I knew my presence would be useful and appreciated. I saw in the papers the names of men I knew admired me, and with whom there had already been some solidarity in thought and action. Besides D'Annunzio, there was Giuriati (who founded the Fascio di Combattimento with me in Rome); there was Host-

Venturi, who I'd seen a month earlier in Milan; there were Marinetti and Vecchi, my dear brothers in arms; there were Keller, Pinna, Cerati, Forti, and Scambelluri, the Futurist vanguard of legionaries. How could I resist such supreme temptation? If I'd happened to have the wings of the young aviators of Aiello, I wouldn't have waited a minute to fly straight to Fiume. But I was behind bars, alone and without help, horribly enchained.

To quell ever so slightly the impatience that was devouring me, I wrote some enthusiastic articles about D'Annunzio, and a proclamation I sent to *L'Ardito*, which the censors redacted completely.

Even today, the ideas expressed therein have the force of life and the value of actuality.

To All the Arditi on Land, Sea, and Air!

Hey!

Men of war, ignorant of defeat!

My knife-wielding, bomb-throwing comrades: on guard!

A new call rings out for all those with Italian guts, hearts, and arms.

Those far away are listening; those not ready are preparing; those ready are taking up arms and waiting.

Quiet now, as I ask you, Arditi:

Victors over the Germans and the Austrians, do you want Italy ruled over once again by the caste of timid, authoritarian old puppets, deniers of liberty and progress of the people?

Do you want to obey once more those ambitious, vile ministers, those pergameneous old senators, those generals concerned only with their careers?

Are you going to allow your nation to be ruled by those who have sucked the best blood of our soldiers, who sold them out and betrayed them, who now want to buy their favor to defend their own bellies?

Scornful, raging Arditi!

The real Italy, the young Italy, the Italy that marches to the front and cuts away all labyrinthine diplomacy with a well-placed dagger stroke, is now in Fiume, in body and spirit.

Know this, Arditi. Fiume today is no longer a city. Fiume is the heart and head of Italy. The strongest, the most brilliant, the most energetic Italians have heeded and hastened to Fiume: the only ones who have the right to lead a proud people.

This city at the apex of our peninsula has become its spiritual center. Heart and head are now one.

Our ancient Rome, asphyxiated by five hundred churches, five hundred ruins, five hundred deputies, and five hundred hotbeds of bureaucracy, should now learn from this lean, charming young city how to love and desire when confronted with overbearing outsiders, and how to govern a nation of intelligent heroes.

Arditi, wipe the rust off the daggers that Chief Nitti hasn't managed to take from you. Heed the call of Fiume.

The cowardly, bone-idle ministers have done nothing but make the crown of their king wobble.

The sophists of all the political parties speculating on human feeling have done nothing but pit Italians against Italians. I want to pit you against those who hate the country and want it weakened, those who are worse than the worst Germans.

Know now that Italy is finally ripe for national revolution. The taking of Fiume is the prologue.

We have the honor of being the ones to achieve this, raking away from our sacred land the bourgeois and proletarian bellies of cowardice, the emasculated flab, the *camorre* who now give orders.[21]

---

[21] The Camorra is an organized criminal association from Campania.

Begin the march, avenging flames, and cry:
"Make way for revolutionary Italy!"

×   ×   ×

Then I secretly wrote to Benito Mussolini, begging him to let me know if he had a way to get me to Fiume without running the risk of getting caught by Nitti's goons. He advised me to avoid Fiume and head to Milan instead, where there was greater need for my work.

Disoriented, but understanding full well that I couldn't stay too long in any city without being arrested, I decided to make a short stop in Milan to connect with Mussolini before proceeding to Fiume. But I didn't have any papers for traveling. How would I get them?

A colleague came to visit me in my silent cave. I asked for the necessary documents to create a new identity, but no one could get them for me. I knew it would be easy to identify me, without some bogus documents of the strictest legality.

From the 20th to the 27th (the day I escaped), I was able to exit my room and potter about in one of the offices, on the pretext of copying out one of my literary works.

During lunch, between twelve o'clock and two o'clock, the offices were almost entirely empty, and the adjutant had promised to let me do some typing in the regimental office itself. The room was a gold mine of documents, and I kept my eye out for just the right moment. Then, one day, I met some unexpected fortune. A typist had left the room, leaving the cabinet with all the depot stamps open.

Making sure that nobody could catch me in the act, I searched the cards scattered on the table and came upon a brand new quinternion of travel papers for officials. I opened the drawer, pulled out the stamps, stamped the pages with scrupulous regularity, pocketed them, and ran to hide them in my briefcase.

Finally!

The next evening, at the hour when the bats come out, as well as the cats in heat and the stars, I tiptoed out of the barracks with a little soldier's cap pulled over my ears, shrouded in the cape of a free and easy infantryman.

At the inn I collected my things, split them among five or six friends, including dear old Mino Soldi who had brought them there, and ran to the station. I was able to leave unseen and reach Milan in peace by eleven o'clock that night.

I had left two letters on my bedroom table: one for my colonel, another for the adjutant. In these letters I said that I couldn't resist the desire to reach Fiume, and urged them not to bother pursuing me because I had left *by air*, and would already be in Fiume by the time they'd begun their search.

In fact, I heard that the depot HQ simply reported the incident to their direct superiors, and didn't lift a finger to track me down.

In Milan I was kept safe, first by one of my devoted friends, then, no longer safe in my friend's house, by the Futurist Mario Dessy at the Hotel Europa. I spent one night in his room, on one of his mattresses on the floor, and ate meals brought up by a waiter with an impetuous, suspicious expression. Of course, the presence of an unknown individual in a guest's room was hardly normal, especially with so little explanation.

Curiosity and doubt began to grow around my person the next day, when I left the hotel room in a picturesque tourist's outfit: gray-green trousers, black and white squared jacket from Settimelli, and a little traveler's beret, brought to me by Armando Mazza.

We entered the hotel's busy courtyard with suitcases and blankets, and set off in a speedy automobile procured by two generous gentlemen. Despite not knowing me, they had kindly offered to provide the means to reach Venice as quickly as possible.

The car journey with my loyal friend the Futurist Mario Dessy, as well as Gianni Caminada, was in fact quite a comedy, not easily forgotten. The chauffeur, like all chauffeurs, had no shortage of blagues, but he mixed them with a loquacity untypical of professional drivers.

The journey was fourteen hours long, during which we had about a dozen breakdowns and various incidents. Trying our best to nap, all we'd hear was the driver's chatter as he animatedly argued with his engine, and his hands polishing the brass at every stop.

In Mestre, we left the car in a garage and took a ferry to Venice. My friends didn't leave me there, since they wanted to see me off to Fiume. We headed to the Albergo della Pace, where we paid rounds for the guests and posed as famous personalities in disguise.

I stayed in Venice for four days, hoping to depart on some steamer heading for Fiume, but the wait was pointless, because there were no departures during that period.

The city of dreams didn't feel especially safe. The archipelago of *calli, campi, campielli, salizzade*, and *fondamenta* was too tight and gossipy,[22] and anyone would quickly become familiar with my face and strange outfit. And when you don't have a clear conscience, you imagine everyone is looking at you suspiciously, and that everyone is ready to report you.

I forced my friends to leave me, and went to hide out in the Corte della Polvere with a lady who rented rooms out to actors. I

---

[22] Narrow streets, squares, small squares, cobbled streets, and canal banks.

passed myself off as a comedy performer who had come to Venice to put together a script during my time off.

Carefully examining the documents proving my new identity (my name was Boveri Umberto, and I'd been discharged for epilepsy), I noticed that all of the physical features corresponded accurately enough with my own, except for the hair, which was blond instead of black.

So I rushed to a perfumer and loaded up on bleaching agents: oxygenated water, chamomile, ammonia. Back home, I patiently and persistently applied them, until my hair started to take on vague tobacco reflections, enough to pose as an authentic blonde.

I also removed my sideburns, which had been one of my distinctive features for years, as well as the white tuft in the middle of my forehead, a source of pride and mark of nobility, for which Settimelli and I had founded the "Sect of the White Tuft." To this day, we are still the only two members.

Thus transformed, my glasses swapped for a monocle, I wandered around Venice, including the lagoon by gondola, until the evening of October 4th, when an Arditi official, Umberto Craighero, convinced me to leave for Ancona, where I was almost certain to find an *MAS* ready to take us to Fiume.[23]

We departed, Craighero and I, with the ever so cheerful and faithful Captain Coletti. I didn't reveal my name immediately. I was Boveri Umberto until we reached the Albergo di Ancona, where I took my captain's uniform from a suitcase and put it on.

When I revealed my identity, I was met with a show of sympathy from both colleagues. There were others there, including Stangher, who tried his best to help us depart. But it was useless: the *MAS* was in storage, the torpedo boats were out of fuel, and the steamers were all manned by Croats who'd hardly be happy

---

23 *Motoscafo armato silurante*: a torpedo-armed motorboat used by the Italian Navy.

to have us aboard.

I couldn't and wouldn't go if I knew I'd be caught. I correctly imagined that the government had already reported my escape to all the coastal bases. So I preferred to make plans in the hotel room with various students from Rome, who dearly desired to be part of Fiume.[24] These included the seventeen-year-old Futurist Elda Norchi, who had boldly run away from home for the noble cause.[25]

Five days and five nights (passed almost entirely by keeping watch, making plans, and drinking cognac) went by without incident. Finally, as all hope seemed lost, discretely disillusioned and disgruntled, we decided to try the land route. On the evening of the 9th we left for Trieste, leaving Norchi and the other students in Ancona.

The train was packed. I spent the night on the floor of a water closet. We reached Trieste without incident on the evening of the 10th, after crossing a large swathe of battlefields, from Treviso to Piave and the Tagliamento, to Udine, Isonzo, Gorizia, Monfalcone, Duino, and finally Trieste.

My emotion reached a peak as we passed through those places where three years of indescribable tortures, dangers, and hardships had been spent, where so much heroism and young blood had been sewn that the earth itself was made supernatural, filled with resounding voices and memories, shudders and sanctity.

It was a brief and purifying journey. We reached beautiful Trieste with serene spirits, and with the desire to make up for lost time and reach Fiume as soon as possible, to add a new spark to the great light that had been lit at Carnaro.

We stayed just one night in Trieste. We were joined by some

[24] "*Fiumanizzarsi*" —Fiumanize themselves.
[25] "Boldly" is given as "*Arditamente.*"

fellow adventurers from Ancona: Lieutenant Zampetti and Captain Lorenzetti, formerly exiled to Switzerland for anti-disciplinary deeds, now back in Italy to become a legionary, wearing a simple soldier's uniform, simulating in exhilarating fashion the poses, gestures, and accent of a common soldier, at once coarse and respectful. We passed him off as our servant, and you should have seen how he filled the role, carrying our multitudinous baggage on his square shoulders, and his triumphant, monumental arrival in Trieste, sitting in a box, while inside the carriage we fell apart laughing.

We hid ourselves in the Hotel Metropole, and let Captain Coletti do all the work, since he was in fact free and on leave. Of the five officials, four were considered deserters, a condition only aggravated for Lorenzetti and I due to our self-administered amnesties from our respective forts.

Not feeling secure in the hotel, I searched for a more trustworthy location. I called on the hospitality of the Lonchar family, of whom I knew Miss Maria in Florence, a cousin of my philosopher friend Augusto Hermet, translator of Novalis.

The Lonchars very kindly agreed to hide me, and I aimed to join them the next morning. But that evening Coletti brought wonderful news to the hotel. Dressed as railway workers, we were going to slip into that city we so desired.

Coletti had made arrangements with Paoloni, director of *Era Nuova*,[26] to whom I'd sent him, and they had put him in touch with Station Master Scocca, one of the most praiseworthy railway men of the Fiume campaign.

On October 11th, at two in the afternoon, I presented myself to Scocca. He had already been informed of my intention to visit.

---

[26] Paoloni had been the chief editor for Benito Mussolini's *Popolo d'Italia* in Rome before being sent to Trieste to run *L'Era Nuova*.

Once he saw me, he called for a typist and told him:

"Make a brakeman card for this gentleman. He needs to get to Fiume."

Then quietly he mumbled:

"This is an important person."

Half an hour later, as the train was setting off, and the watchful eyes of the carabinieri were momentarily averted, I felt the ground move precipitously, and I departed as a package in the baggage car.

Relieved at having defied all the Nittian authorities, I looked around and came to a friendly arrangement with the service personnel.

That day the train was run by Bruni, an estimable man from the Marche, who knew the country, disdained his superiors, and adored everything that smelled of revolution.

Bruni lent me his worker's coat and had a brakeman give me a cap, which fit my now chameleon-like face magnificently.

The diminutive brakeman who gave me his cap refused my offer of some money. Although a little embarrassed by my gaffe, I was proud to wear the uniform of these people, even if only for a few hours.

The journey went peacefully.

Propped up on the baggage-car railing I gazed with moderate intoxication at the rambling, melancholy Karst Plateau, thinking with pulsing desire of all the new engagements, the heroic adventures, the life of passion and poetry awaiting me in Fiume.

I knew that I was bringing a new strength to the young city, already phosphorescent with glorious names and singular characters: I brought my hard, decisive Futurist's mask, which saw in Fiume a luminous anticipation of the future, and my cheerful, colorful aggression, the spirit of a new, fantastic, rebel humanity, which would grab hold of the Carnaro Gulf and launch the most formidable flight for the conquest of Italy and the world.

But since such a task cannot be completed by ten men, and we must accept the competition of some leading faction that is not always chosen, my own idea of Fiume immediately struck the rocks of very different ideas. In Fiume, apart from the combative, clairvoyant, and revolutionary genius of the Commander and a few others, I found far too many elements of the old Italy, of the old traditional mentality, which admitted the D'Annunzian drive without comprehending it and without wanting to extend it. I found careerism and generalism, exhibitionism and profiteering: all far from my idea of renewal that extended the reach of Fiume to phenomena of global interest and a spiritual order.

Meanwhile, the train threaded through the dirty rocks of Istria.

Just before reaching the most dangerous point of the journey, Mattuglie Station, Conductor Bruni said to me: "To avoid arousing suspicion, you'll have to take off your glasses and exit while working like the others."

I obeyed his orders.

I pocketed my glasses, and though barely able to see a thing, I began walking up and down the carriages. On the platform the Nittian carabiniere were strolling about. Every third step I'd walk right into one, shuddering but also laughing to myself at the comedy of the situation.

My fate could be determined by the most minor clue, the slightest doubt, a single distraction.

Would I reach salvation, or would I find myself once again in the claws of reaction that would come down even more proudly this time?

My star was gracious, and the horn announcing the train's departure from Mattuglie echoed through my spirit like the ringing of triumphant liberation, tearing to shreds any phantasms of incarceration.

Finally!

For he who observes the religion of liberty, and adores action more than existence itself, this word holds boundless value.

He who has ever found himself in my condition, in my state of mind, will understand me.

Upon reaching Fiume, I wanted to kneel down and kiss the ground where heroism still had citizenship, and liberty was not a mere word.

Not wanting to plagiarize the D'Annunzians, I did not in fact kiss the earth, but the act was in any case performed in my spirit, and my arms, my gaze, my electrified nerves, my galloping arteries made the sign of expansion and embrace, signifying gratitude, benediction, love, devotion.

From that moment, before even seeing Gabriele D'Annunzio or signing the official oath in the office that received volunteers, I pledged allegiance to Italian Fiume, and to this pledge I know I never gave anything but my all.

FIUMANISM

Is the new postwar religion.

Is the flame that survived the slaughter and decomposition that shattered the consciousness of peoples in search of peace.

Is the tenacious will that renews and perpetuates life, exalting it in the heat of courage and liberty.

Woe to he who remains immune to Fiumanism! The future is not for him.

THE LEADER'S GLORY

"His" Dynasty

The new youth of Fiume blossomed, fragrant with cyclamen, on a pale October morning, which witnessed with an invisible tremor the fast fading, distant boom, and fresh crackle of a monstrous victory.

Fiume is an original girl full of caprice and luminous folly. Spread across the base of the Carnaro, with hair laid along the steps of Abbazia; Fiume, a typical southern, somnolent beauty, lazily falling asleep in midday sun, letting the Hungarian hunters, with their square boots and barbaric, droopy mustaches, do with her magnificent body what predators have always done with their prey.

In truth they were discreet, those powerful magnates who feudalized the lovely sleeper, and used no chains. Perhaps these conquerors hoped the white maiden, upon awaking, between yawns, would throw her arms around the hairy necks of their masculinity.

But *la belle au bois dormant* is awoken to new youth,[27] with a program mysteriously woven through her long medieval slumber. Without the slightest yawn or stretch or flutter of eyelids, she leaps to her feet, limpid and vibrant like the morning of victory, and stretches her arms over the sea with a gesture of both offering and expectation.

Alone on the contested shore, from which the fallen ruler retreated in silence, as the echo of the final battle rumbles on, she awaits the liberator. A polychrome octopus, crawling and murmuring promises of gilded slavery, tries to grab her.

The little one spots the ambush and fights off the hideous tentacles for ten months, desperately calling "Italy! Italy! Italy!"

And behold, a pure warrior of triumphant wing and harmonious song swiftly descends upon the rock to which Fiume was lately chained, smashing with a single blow all the spells, all the traps, all the knots of mercantile rapacity.

It was a gesture of infinite significance. Few understood its scope. But the future would undoubtedly glorify this artist who had smashed the old tables of the law, which until recently rested so heavily upon the tradition of obedience that even the most glorious and illustrious leaders were hamstrung by poverty of thought. That eternal youth who had never seen so clear and far how the war had almost blinded him; that joyful captor of every radiant light of the world, who came to Fiume in a car showered with smiles and clear-eyed cheer; that velvet ruler, who commanded with poetic imagery and earned obedience through nothing but fascination, until death.

He brought to Fiume a sense of personal liberty, spontaneous discipline, spiritual supremacy, and the light, bubbly elegance of

---

[27] Sleeping Beauty.

Italian genius.

I don't know how many grasped this. Certainly, being by his side for just an hour was to imbibe that superior atmosphere of serene clairvoyance, of courtly grace, of youthful joy.

Gabriele D'Annunzio is the first artist, the first Italian of genius to be given the power of governance. It recalls the glorious precedents set by Lamartine and Victor Hugo. It's a sign that we're destined to a more luminous civilization: that which puts intelligence and poetry in command.

These are the first flickers escaping from the mercantile materialism of this fumbling era. It's one of the most tangible victories of the Great War, and perhaps the most radically revolutionary thing it created.

When humanity feels the fascination and imperial power of genius, when it gets close enough to comprehend, it will not hesitate to grant it direction of the republic.[28]

This will be the truly individualist epoch. The ascent of the masses over victoriously resolved economic problems will pull them into the centrifugal development of personality, and—with pacification—into the hot, magnetic light of genius that epitomizes and personifies the race.

Love of art, overflowing endlessly, will make every man the artist of his own life, and the passions that today revolve around money and sex will pour out into color, harmony, balance, discovery, and research—in short, all the games and follies of the intelligence, which are enough to fill a lifetime.

Gabriele D'Annunzio is the initiator of this dynasty of the brilliant, destined to imprint on politics as well as art the new rhythm of a new world heretofore unknown to the crowd: the abyssal and stellar world of the spirit.

---

[28] *"Cosa pubblica,"* Italian for *"Res publica,"* the Latin name of the Roman Republic.

Today Poetry Is in Command

Today, Gabriele D'Annunzio has all of young Italy, ardent and generous, by his side. Of this there can be no doubt. But he would struggle to find, among the huge crowd that cheers him in the open squares, his old public from ten years ago, who discussed him so passionately in the salons, cafés, and theater lobbies. This was a very special public, mostly consisting of aristocrats, snobs, ladies with lapdogs, journalists, and college girls: those who are usually in on every literary trend, and buzz around the great artists like a chattering wasp's nest near candy.

Where is this public now? What are they doing for their idol? I don't know. Today, this public doesn't matter. They've probably turned on the author of *L'Innocente*. Instead of writing fascinating novels and paradoxical tragedies, he became a real soldier, a real patriot, a real man of action. There are many who, over the last four years, considered D'Annunzio finished as a writer, a buried poet, a deserter of art. They turned their backs on him in disdain.

These softies, these snobs, these out-of-touch people are wrong, and I wouldn't even mention them if they didn't reveal something important about the mentality of official Italy. As long as a man is talked about as a writer, as a wild artist, as long as he holds the attention of all the European intellectuals with his verbal edifices, it's all fine: "Bravo! Exceptional! What a great man!" But when this fabricator of thoughts or sentences rises from his desk, dons a uniform, shoulders a weapon, and rushes to realize the images of his spirit, to give life to his phantasms, to translate his poetry into action—well, then, official Italy (its cowardly calculations upset) furrows its brows, scrunches its face in disgust, stamps its feet in rage, and concludes that all this is literature!

Such a powerful example of stupidity.

Take a look at the former defenders of Gabriele D'Annunzio's art. Among the most die-hard were the *Corriere della Sera*, which had a monopoly on his first fruits and exalted him with the pens of Janni and Simoni; and the *Tribuna*, where Rastignac declared himself D'Annunzio's defense lawyer. And now these papers have turned against him: not only for the obvious political motives of conservatism against any revolutionary act, but also due to mentality. It is precisely these papers that represent the tendency of an entire category of people to consider poetry an interesting but inoffensive game, and on no account do they want it to plunge into the core of action, struggle, and life.

According to these limp chatterers, D'Annunzio shouldn't wield anything but a pen. And they say the same of Marinetti, me, and a hundred others. What beastly blindness! They can't comprehend that this second scintillating youth of D'Annunzio is so much more important than the first. He has managed to consolidate the indeterminacy of his literary visions into a forceful drama of reality, in which he, the protagonist, is genuinely prepared to die in the last act, with the perfection of great art.

They can't comprehend that a poet has never been so faithful to his imagination, nor so coherent in the extension of his own books, which no longer suffice, into life itself.

Look at his novels and tragedies. Some of his characters strangely resemble him: Stelio in *Fuoco*, for example, or Alessandro in *Città Morta*, or Andrea Sperelli who dreams of conquering cities, Ruggero Fiamma, or Corrado Brando and his heroism and exceptional audacity.

Who will say that he wasn't meditating on achieving such feats, which he enviously attributed to literary creations, and which current events now allow him to realize?

In any case, one thing is certain: he has succeeded, he has

triumphed. From now on, his *deed* (not his *gesture*,[29] as they call it), his knightly adventure, his enterprise of poetry and justice, is now approved history and exalted legend.

I can solemnly declare, whether against those who admire the poet and ridicule the commander, or against those who glorify him as a soldier and denigrate him as an artist, that there was never a man more suited to command a brilliant and heroic people. The man of war is inspired by a formidable spiritual substance. The man of letters is sustained by great physical courage. From this is born one of the happiest combinations, of the most robust charm, and the most complete of personalities.

This was already known by those who make their grotesque efforts at undermining the man who is now invested with the right to guide the destiny of all of Italy.

D'Annunzio is not a general, yet he has demonstrated the ability to organize and lead troops, flights, and assaults.

He is not a diplomat, yet if he instead of Sonnino and Tittoni headed to Paris,[30] he would have gained Fiume and more without all the torment or bitterness. Those who know him will swear on it.

He is not a politician, and yet he'd be able to govern Italy in a much more civil and enlightened manner than those who currently misrule it.

I know no better expert in men, no better interpreter of souls, no greater lord, no more courageous defender of what he loves. Which Italian politician would ever offer his life for Fiume? D'Annunzio has done it. With D'Annunzio in power, no Wilson and no American bank would have threatened the starvation of Italy.

This Italy that places pride and dignity above hunger does not

---

[29] His "*gesta*," not his "*gesto*."

[30] Sidney Sonnino was the prime minister of Italy in 1906, and again from 1909–1910. Tommaso Tittoni was an Italian diplomat.

want petty, shortsighted administrators as its ministers. Yes, there should be, indeed there *must be* administrators. But a nation, more than just stomachs, also consists of consciences and hearts, and the government of ten million consciences and hearts cannot be entrusted to the shadiest, most shriveled-up accountant's head in the whole country.

This is why we need to break up the powers and responsibilities of government: the administration will be placed in the honest and capable hands of hardworking technicians; above them, the watchful directorate, entrusted to big brains, modern and courageous, dedicated interpreters of the collective consciousness.

Only in this manner are the ideals and interests of a people preserved in harmonious proportions, such that the heart doesn't impose any unnecessary sacrifices on the stomach, and the stomach doesn't stifle the generous impulses of the heart.

Now it is only the purest and most beautiful poetry that commands.

But tomorrow, by its side, without overwhelming or diminishing it, there will be other minor and essential figures to set the superior conquests of poetry in everyday life.

The Velvet Dominion

It is perhaps the first time in the world that the wings of lyricism, like an airplane, recalling rather than contrasting with the facts of reality, manage to establish the harmony of a new rhythm of life, which goes beyond the definitions and distinctions of philosophizers.

The free and distinctively Italian genius of Gabriele D'Annunzio has achieved this feat. Finally, we can breathe.

For four months now in Fiume, thanks to this achievement, we have been able to breathe.

The old antitheses of life and dream, reality and poetry, common sense and imagination, have finally been surpassed. Each term can now be considered fused and superimposed.

All artists, all moderns, all geniuses can join me in singing *alala* for this victory that D'Annunzio has torn from the idiotic and myopic past,[31] which placed so many barriers and prohibitions before the human spirit, under the pretext of differentiation, specialization, and delimitation.

The spirit has escaped through the bars imposed upon it, has multiplied its horizons, is victoriously planted between sky and earth, affirming its right to include in its dominion each of these atmospheres.

Gabriele D'Annunzio brought unique luggage to Fiume, a complete world that no man of politics has possessed before him, and whose transmission will be a delicate and perhaps insoluble problem of human psychology.

Above all, he brought his past as an artist and thinker, for which he enjoyed universal acclaim: an international record as an Italian intellectual. He brought his glory as a mutilated elite soldier, which commanded the respect of all peoples emerging from the war: an international record for Italian heroism. He brought his personal charm, as a man, as a gentleman, and as an expert navigator, which earned him loyal friendships and enthusiastic sympathy: an international record of spiritual magnetism.

With all of this luggage, entirely different from the diplomatic briefcase of some Tittoni,[32] he established his dominion over Fiume. Some fool has called it his "dictatorship," even his

---

[31] "*Alala*" was the personification of the war cry in Greek mythology. D'Annunzio modified it and used it as a war cry.

[32] Tommaso Tittoni, 1855–1931, politician and diplomat, minister of foreign affairs (1903–1905 and 1906–1909), and head of the Italian delegation at the Paris Peace Conference.

"militaristic dictatorship." There's no point in debating. They should step inside the magic circle of D'Annunzian dominion and judge for themselves.

Dominion, yes, absolutely. Everyone obeys the Commander, but joyfully, pulsating with love, as one would obey the orders of an alluring woman. You just need to reach the threshold of his refuge (Workroom? Parlor? Cabin? Command deck? How to describe it?) and receive a smile, an autograph, an order, a word, praise or admonition, no matter, once you manage to brush against his aura, inhale the outer extremities of his intense spirituality, you will leave with that intimate intoxication that only the presence of saints can provoke, which releases a sense of sacrifice and heroism even in egotistical and cowardly natures.

Whoever claims to see *only* the poet, or *only* the statesman, or even *only* the man, has a limited vision of the "phenomenon." The interpenetration of these elements (lyricism, wisdom, common sense, leadership, and personal charm) is precisely what characterizes his personality.

Among his legionaries, he has been able to live all lives, enter all souls, mold himself to all uniforms, exalt every source of pride, unbridle every virtue. In his "close relationships" he wears a humble Arditi uniform, with no rank or decoration. He has spoken with at least one hundred officials, and many rowdy and outspoken soldiers, in the same gracious tones he would have used with a group of nobles in a salon.

None of the strutting, austere, and cretinous rigidity of the usual "close relationships" maintained by careerist generals, those massive inciters of collective yawns and ferocious irritation. No regulations, no circulars, no playground "morals," but rather the swift, human, clairvoyant word of a man of thought and energy, who can command with a simple request and has no need to raise his voice to gain obedience.

Among the soldiers, who tear themselves apart to stand next to him, he had a profound sense of psychology. He found the words and gestures that reached the heart in magnificent harmony, and often enough the guts, which were kept in excellent condition.

His *Compagnia Disperata* called him *caporale*.[33] He sipped shots in saintly peace with their leader, who once reproached him for caring so much about governance that he couldn't take proper care of his squadron.

And the *Ignoranti* Unit, commanded by the most ignorant Captain Argentino, declared that D'Annunzio came first, then God, then the captain.

Invited to mess one morning by the Alpini, he sat with them quietly and ate the whole meal from his new mess tin, slicing the bun like an authentic trooper and drinking like an authentic Alpine soldier.

Yet there are still those who talk of aestheticism, of artificial mannerisms, and medieval ceremonialism. There is nothing of the sort. Everything is vitalized by the air of new life, and ceremony is nothing but a way to communicate with the people and the soldiers. Aesthetics, which are unavoidable, are vivified by a powerful breath of humanity. An original aristocracy blooms from the thousands of buds of all the lives he has lived, and his machine-gunners' motto, *"me ne frego,"* takes on the quality of a heroic

---

[33] The "desperate battalion" was D'Annunzio's bodyguard unit. These young soldiers had arrived to Fiume without documents, and were turned away by headquarters. They camped in Fiume's naval yards. According to Giovanni Comisso, when D'Annunzio's close friend Guido Keller paid them a visit, he was impressed by their "drunk and happy" energy, and decided to make them D'Annunzio's bodyguards. *"Caporale"* primarily means "corporal," but can also mean "foreman," or an illegal employer of day laborers.

legend, like the *"Merde!"* of the French marshal.[34]

This is not literature, my dear Italians! Every word of Gabriele D'Annunzio's declarations is a cry of Fiuman passion. Every lyrical flight corresponds to a real and even tragic flight of one of our aviators. Every little dig is matched by an act of genuine energy. The *Cagoietti* received more than one example of this.[35]

Among those of us who have proven our loyalty to the best among today's Italians, there is more than one who has seen in the taking of Fiume not only a work of justice and Italianity, not only the defense of a dear, martyred city against a *trust* of ravenous predators, but also and above all the first appearance in Italy of a new form of existence, the first realization of a dream of rebellion that was waiting impatiently for the right hour and the occasion to give a monumental kick to a thousand moldy traditions and all the junk laws, to all the outdated ideas and attitudes that still govern the old Italy.

We are now the unique inheritors of the revolutionary sense of the war, and we declare that our rebellion of exiles is the only genuinely Italian revolutionary act of the post-war period.

Italians of the other shore, we also work for you, and also to give you a more noble, more intelligent, more modern country, that we linger in the rough gray-green of war. All the worse for you if you don't understand this. We know your obtuse misery can do nothing but slander. While we, day by day, give you lessons in greatness, you become even greater philistines. You're like those petit-bourgeois who rail against the large fashion houses,

---

[34] *Me ne frego,* "I don't give a damn," or "I don't care," is an Italian fascist slogan. Pierre Cambronne, the Napoleonic general who Carli refers to here, reportedly responded to his British rival Sir Charles Colville's demand for surrender with *"merde!"* ("Shit!")

[35] *Cagoia,* "snail" in Triestine dialect, was D'Annunzio's name for Francesco Saverio Nitti, prime minister of Italy between June 1919 and June 1920.

which their little purses can't afford.

But one thing is certain: that if in this *incagoiata* and bestial Italy you want to find some trace of the new spirit, it's to Fiume, and only to Fiume, that you need to come.

D'Annunzio at the Rally

For the first time, Gabriele D'Annunzio held an electoral rally. It was an interesting event from all points of view. D'Annunzio is a poet, a man of war, a raiser of consciousness, and a driver of the will. But until now, we have not known him as a politician, as a president of electoral assemblies.

Yesterday evening, at the Teatro Verdi, he revealed himself as an expert political orator. He tapped the most sensitive keys of the collective soul, without sliding into the clichés of demagogy and courtierism deployed by the flatterers of crowds. He pulled all of Fiume along, affirming, repeating, promising, and swearing whatever he wanted.

It was like a rapid-fire dialogue between himself and the public. I don't know if there was more iron force in his questioning, or more joyful obedience in the responses. Over and over, they declared their desire to be Italians, nothing but Italians, and their intention to vote in the elections.

The constituency was large, and the shrill voices mixed with baritone men became an energetic symphony, like a marching fanfare. Once more, as if it was necessary, we saw how D'Annunzio was idolized, and how the idea of the country, for everyone in Fiume, was now identified with his name.

You should have heard the mighty "Yes!" from their chests at each of the Commander's questions. If ever it was appropriate to talk of the multitude's frenzy for one man, this was the time. The fascination of this little white lancer of sober gesture and articulated words, this elegant, mutilated Italian whose chest couldn't fit all his medals for bravery, was such that a smile, or a mere wave of an ungloved hand (as small as that of Napoleon) sufficed to unchain the crowd's frenzy. It might be said that last night this frenzy in the form of applause, ovation, shouts, and flowers reached the point of suffocation.

It seemed like the crowd wanted to embrace their liberator, drawing him further and further into a hurricane of passionate enthusiasm. Now and then it seemed his genial, illuminated face was submerged in the rising tide of white-hot screams, only to re-appear in the wave of heads and smiles that incited new outpour-ings and new polyphonic squalls.

The rally came to a most excellent end, full of Futurist flavor, with the Commander inviting Fiumans to swap the old slogan "It-aly or death!" for "Italy and life!"

Fiume, October 28th.

D'Annunzio's Futurism

One evening, in the main theater of Fiume, I yelled that Ga-briele D'Annunzio, as a prodigious builder, was an authentic Fu-turist.

There were some who scoffed at this, and those who found it insulting to the Commander.

He himself, on the other hand, understood that this wasn't a declaration to be taken lightly. He recognized the undeniably Fu-turist side to his temperament, even if such "isms" were an ephemeral terminology that designate a necessary battle, which become exhausted and give way to other struggles under other names. In Futurism, he nevertheless saw the tireless will to re-newal of human thought, constructing new modes and rhythms of art and life.

In D'Annunzian poetry, among the clouds of homage to the past, sparkle magnificent lights of the future, the anticipations and prophecies of an avant-garde mind, which has filled its age with rockets and lightning flashes.

His life itself has been nothing but a series of Futurist deeds, pioneering and innovative, the value of which we deeply appreciate. His spirit is always listening for the new voices that spring from our land, and all the forces that stir obscurely in the world in search of expression. His motto, "renew or die,"[36] is exquisitely, heroically Futurist. The other more recent motto, "I don't plot, I dare,"[37] is an affirmation of Futurism. There is tangible Futurism in the proud anti-renunciation "Lettera ai Dalmati," and the marvelous *Disobbedisco,*[38] in which the Garibaldian phrase is inverted with daring wit.[39]

The Commander's Lyrical Teas

On Sunday, in armed and vigilant Fiume, he allows himself an hour of rest and serene joy.

For an hour each Sunday, the man who sleeps three hours a night, and has worked fifteen hours a day for the last five and a half months, receives in his lounge the intimate and the faithful, or some native authorities, some local nobility or an artist, for a sober tea, a harmonious baby grand, purple flowers, and exquisite words.

---

[36] *O rinnovarsi o morire.*

[37] *Ardisco non ordisco.*

[38] The "Lettera ai Dalmati," or "Letter to the Dalmatians," was written by D'Annunzio.

[39] "I disobey." In 1866, during the Third Italian War of Independence, after an armistice was announced between Austria and Italy, Garibaldi famously responded to an order to abandon Trentino with one word: *"obbedisco"* — "I obey."

Those who write have always hated salons, whether aristocratic or bourgeois, whether entirely frivolous or with literary pretensions. But, when D'Annunzio is there, the salon is no longer a salon; it's a station of the spirit, from which tracks of fantastic imagery run, tangled cables buzz with thought, mysterious signals light up, where all the trains of intelligence merrily rush, flowering with rockets and fragrant branches. It's especially sweet, in these wakeful breaks in aggressive ardor, to linger in the warm room whose windows look down on the quiet port and outstretched piers, leading the nostalgic senses to imagine some distant Roman winter, full of byzantine splendors and cerebral subtleties.

But here in the air itself there's something that cautions, and never lets you forget the present of passionate metallic tensions that pervade everyone and everything.

On the coffee tables, amid bunches of carnations blood-red like the flag of Zara, were albums and illustrated books on Fiume, Dalmatia, and the islands. In one corner there's a shining silk pennant, adorned with an appealing motto. The conversations are vibrations of love for the martyred cities, glimpses of combative pride and vivacity, at once echoes and anguishes of battle.

All of a sudden, over the tumult of words and witty crossfire, the sedative wave of melody glides, and there is silence. Then the building lights up with sound like some divine intruder taking all one's attention and canceling all other thought.

Luisa Bàccara sits at the fortepiano with her metallic attire and hair that breathes.[40]

There are those who watch the powerful worker as she untangles with long-honed skill the sounds that have been caught in the darkness of the keys, during the long hours of enclosed silence.

---

[40] Luisa Bàccara was a mistress of D'Annunzio.

Notice that she plays not only with her soul, and not only her whole vibrating body, but that there are immediate correspondences between the keys and her melodic vertebrae, which are seen vibrating lower or higher, depending on the key.

Notice that the hands reflected in the upturned ebony lid seem like the hands of a mysterious demon, hidden in the trapezoidal body of the piano. And the music, in fact, through those rhythmic, vibrating hands, has the substance of an ebony abyss, full of dusky reflections sharply zigzagging inside the absurd frame imposed upon the most perfect of instruments by its mad inventor.

The listeners, in a silent circle, assume "interesting" poses. A young official with a Dostoyevskian beard, sunk into an armchair as if it was a sitz bath, clasps his knees with his meshed hands, and assumes an absorbed air worthy of a figure in Balestrieri's "Beethoven." The cheeks of a young Belgian diplomat, ultra-intellectual and modern, turn more pale with each fluctuation in the music. A lady from Fiume, married to a sympathetic journalist, shakes her mantle of black curls to the rhythm of the sonata, accompanying the notes like fraternal bells. A general with the face of a wise and skeptical archdeacon seems to recline voluptuously in the soft hammocks woven by the sounds. A little colonel, serious and sure of himself, eyes the musician and instrument with the look of a satisfied butler. Another colonel snorts and looks down from his half-lens glasses at the music he doesn't appear to enjoy.

Occasionally, the white jacket of a zealous waiter cuts the threads of meditation and spiritual absorption like a shutter of intrusive white lead. But the curved artist doesn't see or know. All her energy is spent separating and untangling the muscular knots of the composition, like a warrior clutching the hair of a tamed enemy.

Indeed, as the divine Ariel put it,[41] "When the strong hands have ceased to draw from the keyboard the maximum resonance, as if from a compressed orchestra, at the point where fullness thins out into a pure melodic design, the musician loosens the arch of her neck and the force of her shoulders with a breath, lifting her face and tilting it backward."[42]

These are the Commander's lyrical "teas."

The Italian Regency of Carnaro

A Work of Art

From the deepest roots of the Italian soul flows this latest incarnation of healthy, happy, and harmonious universality to which our race tends.

Only the Italian people are capable of expressing the miracle of this synthesized man, whether artist or diplomat, soldier or orator, sportsman or prophet, military leader or legislator.

At a later date, I'll provide an analysis of the Regency of Carnaro statutes, which were inspired and dictated by the superior intelligence of Gabriele D'Annunzio, assisted by the political wisdom and experience of Alceste de Ambris.[43]

Today I'll simply affirm that they are D'Annunzio's masterpiece: a work of art consisting of life and humanity, adhering to life and humanity, full of luminous openings to the future, that Gabriele D'Annunzio wants to give to Italy as his magnificent, definitive gift.

---

[41] D'Annunzio was sometimes called Ariel, after the character in Shakespeare's *The Tempest*.

[42] From "Ritratto di Luisa Baccara," an essay by D'Annunzio published in *La Vedetta d'Italia*, February 20th, 1920.

[43] Alceste De Ambris was a revolutionary syndicalist.

This work is the radiant summation of all his lyrical and con-
structive energy. It is worth all the tormented passion that this
prodigious life couldn't satisfy with written dramas and poems,
but had to pour into tangible creations molded from the soul and
daily suffering of a people.

The creator is revealed in this delicate embroidery of social
equilibria, where the most ancient traditions, renewed with the
sincere breath of modernity, are reaffirmed as fundamental
schema of the bloodline's continuation.

This creation is in fact the hot breath of life, realized in its most
sublime daring, and Fiume will be the first city in the world where
such blocks of new life are tested.

For me, a fervent believer in the supreme and victorious function of art in the existence of peoples, there is no section of this
constitution more beautiful, more just, more practical, than that
concerning music.

Marinetti too, in his manifesto "Beyond Communism," tried to
lyrically resolve the tangle of political and social problems by the
flooding of every human spirit with art, especially music.

"Music will reign over the world," wrote Marinetti. "Every
square will have its great instrumental and vocal orchestra. There
will be fountains of harmony, from which musical genius will
flow day and night, flowering in the sky to color, ennoble, rein-
vigorate, and refresh the hard, dark, beaten, and convulsive
rhythm of everyday life. Instead of night work, we have night art.
Squads of musicians will alternate to multiply a hundredfold the
splendor of daytime and the sweetness of night."

And here is what Fiume's legislator solemnly declares:

"In the Italian Regency of Carnaro, music is a social and religious institution. If every rebirth of a noble people is a lyrical effort, if every unanimous and creative sentiment is a lyrical power,
if every new order is a lyrical order in the vigorous sense of the

word, then music, considered as a ritual language, exalts the act of life, the work of life."

And further:

"In all the municipalities of the regency, there are choral and instrumental bodies subsidized by the state."

Thus the great pioneering spirits rub shoulders while divining the truth and seizing for our era the sparks of the incandescent sun of the future.

This is how Italy is shown the interpretation of its new life.

Will Italy comprehend and assimilate?

The Legislator

Three fundamental characteristics should be highlighted in these statutes. Without exaggeration, these have baptized Gabriele D'Annunzio's masterpiece:

1. The absolute supremacy of the individual spirit, tireless creator of new works and new appearances, over the heavy immobility of human history. This spiritual individualism is not closed up in egoistical armor, separating and preserving it from all contact, but is outstretched to give, to raise up, to transfigure other lives, to construct a more complete and noble expression of humanity.

2. The prodigious modernity of vision, which shows how his pioneering genius is almost exhausted trying to contain himself in immediate reality and in the assimilative possibilities of his time, in order to avoid spilling out into the unexplored sea of the future. Despite this heroic virtue of constitution and limitation, he has still managed to provide a deeply new and young law, which will be received with shock and joy by the people in the hinterland of Fiume, and all those Italians ripe

for the new earthly dawn.

3. An extremely high and broad sense of human dignity, according to which it is not enough to provide daily bread to all men and women. The bread of the soul, of conscience and right, shared in equal proportions among those who work and build, is essential. All civil and military legislation, more or less hypocritically, treats the human masses as flocks without will or dignity. Gabriele D'Annunzio instead treats the element of *man* with a deep respect, whether in his collectivity or in his individuality.

This will be his immortal glory. More than anything, it is from this comprehension of men and their time, this respect for beauty and the value of every life, that the stream of magnetic sympathy that miraculously envelops the Commander flows.

The obtuse conservatives persist with the brutal and imbecilic rhetoric of anti-demagoguery to pour scorn on these expressions and apparitions of humanity, which have nothing to do with their congregation, sect, or party.

Gabriele D'Annunzio is the only Italian today who, beyond parties and class hatred, managed to create the miraculous formula reconciling patriotic idealism and racial pride with human and social reason.

To those who, despite these immense proofs of disinterest, generosity, and greatness, continue to insult and defame him, we say with the certainty of indisputable prophecy:

"The day will come when all the parties of Italy, and all the social classes, will glorify his name like that of a great liberator: as he who not only liberated Fiume from all oppression, but most importantly Italy from the most tragic shackles of spirit and substance."

To the commander and legislator of Fiume, *glory*!

ARDITISM OF WAR AND ARDITISM OF PEACE

Speech delivered in the Verdi Theater in Fiume, to the Arditi of the 8th, 13th and 22nd divisions, and to the citizens of Fiume, on the evening of October 27th, 1919.

My role this evening, dear *Fiumani*, is to simply present a new form of art, which the Arditi 8th division wanted to share with you for the first time: *Synthetic Futurist Theatre*.

But since this spectacle has been set up to celebrate the anniversary of Vittorio Veneto, and particularly the Battle of Sernaglia, in which the 8th division shined with the brightest valor, allow me to speak a little of the Arditi, my most intense pride and joy, the Arditi, loved by you, oh *Fiumani*, though you may not know much about them.

Last year, the Battle of Vittorio Veneto didn't just decide the fate of Italy. It was also a victory for everyone opposed to the imperialist coalition threatening to submerge the freedom of all Latin peoples.

The part played by the Arditi in that battle was so conspicuous and brilliant that General Zoppi—who nowadays, driven by careerism, heaps scorn on the Fiume crusade—remarked in his agenda:

> It was you who opened the most important door to today's victories. On the night of the 26th, crossing the Piave with yearning souls and pockets full of petards, you advanced on the enemy, and everything depended on you.
>
> Italy, faithful though tense, followed in the wake of your ships and listened out for the first roar of arms. The first explosion in the insidious gloom of the opposite shore was immense, sacred, and solemn like the voice of God. It was the first principle of the new story of Italy.

Despite his limitless praise, despite the fact that the Arditi merited, as the supreme commander said in his encomium, *national recognition*, a month after the armistice the Arditi were disbanded by General Zuppelli, with precipitous urgency, and the *black, red, and green flames* were scattered in a chaos of depots, almost like the wreckage of some military disaster. Thus a silent campaign of political and bureaucratic conspiracies, to the detriment of the Flame of Italy, obtained a momentary success. Italian Bolshevism, which saw in every veteran—not without reason—*an enemy,* sneered in satisfaction because the Arditi, those fearful avengers of Caporettist defeatism, were no longer around. [44]

Oh, how the depot commanders rushed to rip the flames from

---

[44] The Battle of Caporetto (or the Twelfth Battle of the Isonzo), October 24th through November 19th, 1917, has been described by Brian R. Sullivan as "the greatest defeat in Italian military history."

our collars, the decorations from our arms, and insolently do up our jackets. I heard that an official in one depot told an ex-Arditi, "Button up that jacket! Only drunks leave their jackets open!"

In Rome, on the Corso, a celebrated photographer was even prohibited from exhibiting a photo of an Arditi sergeant, as if it was an act of public indecency! As for me, I was arrested a good number of times because—wanting to console my comrades in arms facing national ingratitude—I wanted to reunite them under a different form, and founded the Associazione fra gli Arditi d'Italia, which thrives today and counts thousands of members. And finally, when that city suffocating under five hundred churches, five hundred bureaucratic covens, and five hundred deputies, wanted to pay tribute to the returning troops, the Arditi received the supreme insult and the supreme honor of being left out of the festivities. And I, who yelled in the public squares that the Arditi could do without the flowers and applause of draft dodgers, since they fought for the glory of Italy, not for the recognition of little old official Italy, received ministerial thunderbolts and was removed from Rome.

Today, finally, in Italy's Fiume, by will of the most Arditi of the Arditi, and by the generosity of Commander D'Annunzio, not only do the Arditi have their place in the sun and anywhere else where there are risks to be taken, they have also received that ideal reward they'd so dreamed of. The black ribbon now pinned to our chests, that little stripe the color of death, that the ministers of war, from their perch of governmental stupidity, had always denied us, now without difficulty, without bureaucratic manipulation, has been granted to us by the Commander, in exchange for the knife patch we gave to all the soldiers of Fiume.

From now on our insignia of every color are called Knights of Death. Nothing is more lovely or terrible than this title. Each of us holds it as the dearest decoration and most beautiful memento of our voluntary service.

Last night, I presented the Arditi with the general outline of the civilian program for peace time. Allow me to discuss them.

×   ×   ×

Arditism, a quality revealed on a grand scale by the war, and which is not a monopoly of our corps, but of all the new Italian youth, holds the same function in our time that romanticism held a century ago. Arditism, let us remember, is not only the ability to perform acts of military valor; it is not only that aptitude which is revealed in frontal assaults and hand-to-hand combat, and which is celebrated by a blue ribbon or some solemn commendation. It is above all a tendency of the spirit, a mainspring of character, a constant attitude of the human personality, which reveals itself in a hundred ways under a hundred different forms.

Great young nations are by instinct, and have a duty to be, physiologically and morally daring.[45] A people can have faith in their future only when they are constantly inspired in their ideas and actions by a daring that must not be without shrewdness and common sense.[46] This daring, this faculty and will to *dare*,[47] is revealed in every manifestation of its life: in work, in commerce, in politics, in art, in social life—wherever there is a choice to be made between a mediocre, prudent, narrow-minded, and tranquilizing decision, and a bold, ingenious, and farsighted decision.

The Arditi epitomized and personified this tendency during the war, and for this reason they constitute a symbol or exponent of the mass of fighters.

Tomorrow they will have to propagate among our people that

---

[45] "Daring" here is "*ardite*."

[46] "Daring" here is "*ardimento*."

[47] "To dare" here is "*osare*."

sense of personal responsibility and aggression in struggle that made them magnificent soldiers and hardened them for all the trials of existence. This boldness that made them run singing and joking in the midst of machine-gun fire, that pulled precious words like ruby reds from the lips of the dying, that had them launch like leopards and gave them sublime ferocity—they will now have to apply this daring to a new way of life, to peacetime. No more daggers, no more hand grenades, no more ferocity. Life may be a battle, from the first day to the last, but the qualities, means, and methods of struggle vary. From the atmosphere of war it is essential to preserve precisely that spirit of throbbing intoxication that enables us to face all obstacles, dangers, and sufferings victoriously.

Arditism of war and Arditism of peace: there is a difference. A year ago, in Rome, in Milan, in Turin, in Genoa, in Reggio Emilia, when the Arditi started taking to the public squares, led by their officers, taking the black pennant wherever any word of Italianity needed to be affirmed, wherever victory needed to be defended and integrated with the annexation of Fiume and the Dalmatian cities, there was Arditism of peace. During those rallies where our mere presence imposed holy terror on the square, already forgetful of victorious Italy, there was Arditism of peace. When we arrived in Fiume, to give this divine city all our youth that had survived one hundred battles, there was Arditism of peace.

Speaking the truth wherever it is useful and dangerous, confronting hostile crowds, forgoing pleasure, comfort, luxury, to defend an idea, accepting jail and exile for the sake of justice, refusing shelter to risk an adventure everyone calls mad, adopting iron discipline, but ready to disobey when obedience means renouncing the ideal: here, O Fiumans, are a few ways to describe Arditism in civil life.

It must inform the whole future; it must color the work and

thought of Italians young and old with magnificence; it must be the signal and watchword for every movement of the collective and individuals. The Arditi tendency has the eyes of all Italy upon it. It is what inspired our great chief in the taking of Fiume. All this is expected of us, all illumination, gestures, resolutions, the possible and the impossible, the most soaring lyricism, and the most muscular practicality.

We are the ones who can work quietly and act lightning-fast. We let out our cry when we have the hem of victory's robe in our claws. Nothing is too immense or audacious to frighten us. No difficulty discourages us.

Were we ordered tomorrow to plant the tricolor in all the cities of Dalmatia, we would go, hawkeyed, with wolf-like steps and unerring claws. Black, proud, silent, a rustling in the night, a leap, a flash, a roar, and an impulsive *alala*: done!

Were we ordered tomorrow to capture Cagoia and bring him skewered like a skillfully browned piglet, we would do it without a moment's hesitation.

The day before yesterday, when a leader of the Fiume Armed Forces told the class of 1894 and 1895 that they could, if they wished, return to their homes, an icy silence greeted the announcement. When the leader invited all those who asked for leave to come out from the ranks, not one moved. Serious, calm, self-confident, they declared without hesitation their unchanging destiny to remain at Fiume's disposal until the complete resolution of the fifteenth battle,[48] until inevitable victory. This example, O legionaries of Fiume, deserves to be followed.

Here, meanwhile, is immediate evidence of civilian Arditism. Arditism in the artistic field—Futurism. Tonight, for the first time,

---

[48] A reference to the Second Battle of the Piave River (June 15th to June 23rd, 1918), a key victory against Austria-Hungary.

Fiumans attend a performance of Futurist theater.

Our friends in the 8th Unit had a bold and sympathetic initiative. Did you want proof that Arditism and Futurism are related, if not identical terms? Well, here it is. These Arditi, who are not part of the Futurist movement, nor authors of the works performed, wanted to put on a daring show,[49] so they had no other choice but Futurist theater. Their choice was spontaneous, from instinctive sympathy, without any Futurist influencing their decision. I didn't know until the night before last.

And now I will introduce tonight's performance.

Now the floor is given to the performers who are now doubly Arditi, because they are dealing with Futurism, a terrible powder keg of ideas.

But before I retire, I invite you, O Fiumans, to throw a triple *alala* to that great and authentic Futurist, Commander Gabriele D'Annunzio.

---

[49] "Daring" here is "*ardita.*"

WE FILIBUSTERS

The Caporettist generals, like Nigra,[50] thrown at the blockade lines by the ministers who give amnesty to deserters, slyly adorned with the name of a hero of Vittorio Veneto or some other illustrious leader, have managed to create delightful legends about us legionaries and given us graceful titles that we'll jealously guard with all the other bounty of our endeavor.

To discredit us in the eyes of soldiers still hesitating on the trail of traditional obedience, or to ward off any action that would smash the old codes and prohibitions, they have painted us in the most injurious colors, with no lack of Garibaldian flavor. Repeated by philistine journals like the *Corriere della Sera* and anti-Italian politicians like Modigliani, they haven't failed to have

---

[50] General Arturo Nigra, who strongly opposed the Fiume enterprise. He was captured by legionaries and brought to Fiume in January 1920. See *The First Duce: D'Annunzio at Fiume* by Michael A. Ledeen, page 157.

some impact among the oh-so-moral Italian bourgeoisie, always scandalized by the slightest thing—except their own disease—and always ready to see a bandit in every Ardito, a "filibuster" in every hero.

Yes, they've really called us "filibusters."

They've described Fiume as a forge of sin.[51] They've painted us as a gang of bandits, on whose heads rests a massive bounty, and who, sooner or later, will find themselves in Sussak or Cantrida, with their wrists cuffed together by Cagoia's carabinieri.

But since absurdity can't simply spread with impunity, and even the policeman-minister has unofficially praised the legionaries, the initial insult has been diluted into one remaining word: "adventurers."[52]

And the insult deepens instead of subsiding.

While the first aimed to tarnish our social image, figuring us as predators or unscrupulous fighters, with the second they aim to stain our purity, our disinterestedness, our spotless profile as defenders of the free will of the people.

Faithful to our motto, we don't pay much attention to this pseudo-distortion, which would only influence superficial or small-minded, timorous spirits.

Instead we're happy to wear the words of our defamers, like an enemy arrow transformed into a badge of honor. Adventurers? Filibusters? Our adventure is so beautiful, generous, and new, that such epithets don't bother us.

Is it not perhaps our spirit of adventure, infinitely superior to all of your careerist officials who, under the pretense of maintaining discipline, remained on "the other side" to preserve their dusty epaulets or pensions?

---

[51] *"Delitto."*

[52] *"Avventurieri."*

Is our conscious disobedience not greater, more luminous, more heroic than all your unconscious discipline, consisting of regulations and pedantry, tradition and fear, the unending fear of your superiors?

In this hour of Italian passion and drama, we pride ourselves in representing the true Italy, the new Italy, the young Italy, which was adventurous because it played with its life and power in the tremendous adventure of war, and was called filibustering (that is, imperialistic) by those who wanted at all costs to invest their dollars in an invariably bitter Adriatic.

Words don't impress us; definitions don't disturb us. We know who we are and we know what we want.

We know that many of us, in coming to Fiume, left behind jobs we will never get back, and businesses that will never again prosper. We know that many of us were brutally mistreated by the war, and yet wanted to drag our mutilated bodies all the way to Carnaro—a good example of energy and faith for the intact and the lazy. We know some who abandoned glory more easily obtained in the other camp, to enlist in our ranks as mere grunts.

If some have deviated, if others have betrayed us, who cares? They are punished by their own disgrace, which forced them to flee even from old Italy, when they were not nabbed by our own just and selective justice.[53]

The gates of Fiume were and are all too open, despite the blockade. Those who came to cheat or spy or betray found them left wide open by subtle governmental trickery. We can easily respond to our calumniators that delinquent behavior has never been so actively encouraged by a government. So many spies dressed as legionaries, so many police officers wearing the Arditi uniform, passing through the lines with impunity, who came to

---

[53] *"Giusta giustizia selezionatrice."*

cast upon the pure face of Fiume the obscene freckles of pollution.

But all that has now been identified, and fades away like some malefic abortion before the open flame of our inextinguishable ardor. What remains, which is neither changed nor lost, in time and space, that which we created, simply by having come to Fiume and remained here, is the "Fiuman spirit": *Fiumanism*.

That is, the spirit that has animated our enterprise, and which is neither transitory, ephemeral, nor provisional. Like Arditism, it sprung directly from war, and it cannot die.

The Fiuman spirit and Arditism coincide in contempt for danger and high idealism.

Because this is certain: the Fiume problem will be resolved sooner rather than later. Fiume will have what it has so ardently desired. The right of this people will one day be officially recognized, *but the Fiuman spirit will remain,* and it will manifest in other glorious constructions, and will spread throughout the world, bringing renewal and rebellion wherever there is an injustice to right, a waning old world to topple, a suffocating, organized "trust" to demolish.

Today we can affirm without hesitation that Fiume is the spiritual apex of Italy, because only in Fiume is liberty more than a mere word, and courage more than a legend, faith more than an illusion, and the scent of sacrifice blends miraculously with the scent of youthful audacity, impudent and tuneful.

OUR BOLSHEVISM

And since this is not the hour to fear the sound of certain scare-crow-words, and it's always so enjoyable to eviscerate the pulp that nestles beneath a rind that bristles with deceptive spines, let's confront the old problem of Bolshevism in the Arditi fashion.

×   ×   ×

February mornings on the Carnaro are marvels of azure rays speckled with clouds of pink almond trees, like young flesh climbing up the walls to pick the first fruits and invent imaginary hunts. The roads that rise from the sea to the last Carsic hills, somewhere between the spectral gray of dawn and the mysterious violet of dusk, have a lucidity that promises readiness to unwind with compliant grace under the march of the reddest banners and most formidable vanguard. With eyes of spring, we salute with steadfast optimism even the cruelest inventions of collective fear, and faithfully touch the sunny color of the nocturnal cloak that had made the specters appear so white and terrifying.

From Fiume, an observatory positioned closer to the Orient than Rome or Milan, we can say that the devil is not as black or unaesthetic as it would seem. It's a question of vision and mental serenity, to put it simply.

×   ×   ×

But for there to be no misunderstanding, certain principles must be asserted with unwavering resolve—principles that will never, I presume, be reversed.

In any case, Bolshevism does not coincide with Italian *pussismo*.[54] Taking Russia as a typical model of social revolution, we see, first and foremost, that Bolshevism was less a movement that selfishly expropriated, and more a movement that brought renewal, because it sought to reconstitute the social edifice on the basis of broad, profound ideals—a social edifice which was absurdly lopsided under the decrepit tsarist regime.

What's more, Russian Bolshevism, animated by a powerful breath of mysticism, didn't proceed according to the criteria of cowardly pacifism, which turned Italy's proletarian marches into processions of innocent little lambs, horrified by the sight of blood, yet proudly displaying the crimson carnation in their lapels. The Russian people also knew how to defend their revolution, and Lenin's troops have usually been victorious against the White paladins of reaction.[55]

---

[54] A term derived from *pusillanimità* (pusillanimity), used by Mussolini to describe the cowardice of the Italian Socialist Party.

[55] The White movement was a confederation of anti-Communists in the Russian Civil War.

Given that the Italian socialists do not believe in revolution, do not want it, and will do nothing to provoke it, we can definitively state that we legionaries have no contact with that obtuse, pigheaded, mean-spirited, and cretinous church that is the official Italian Socialist Party. For never accepting the war of rebellion against the Central Powers and continuing to defame it, for having helped Nitti assassinate victory, and for failing to understand the beauty and revolutionary portent of D'Annunzio's enterprise, they are guilty.

×   ×   ×

So it's not to the west that we look when talking about Bolshevism, but to the east.

In every life of a man or people, after a juvenile period of stormy tumult comes the period of wisdom and settling down. After the fever of subversive convulsion, inevitable in any movement of such magnitude, and after the last efforts of reaction have been swept aside, Russia will regain its peace, begin its gradual resurrection, and resume business and intellectual relations with the world at large.

The bloodshed, which seemed so unjust, the mass shootings, the violent repression that brings Lenin close to Marat, will also come to an end, and the Russian people, the most tormented of modern peoples, will have a new life and glory secured for the centuries to come.

It is from this point in the rhythmic process of the Russian Revolution, and from this phase in the Bolshevik disease, that we should depart. Today begins the Russian people's convalescence. Looking back, we recall all the errors and horrors, all the misery and heroism, all the light and shadow through which this people has passed. Their experience is tragic, yet full of vital juices for the future of other peoples. Studying the open wounds of this sublime patient, we can learn how to avoid their errors and integrate the results of their laborious healing process. This is how we will know how to proceed, what precautions to take and obstacles to avoid, so that the scalpel will slice, amputate, and cut with more certainty, straight down without hesitation.

×   ×   ×

We of the socialist mentality are also repulsed by the mania for leveling. Not content with equalizing the initial balance of every purse, they also want to challenge the primacy that intelligence incontestably merits. They would cancel the beauty of the world, making it subservient to immediate utility, without knowing how to create any new form of beauty, and without knowing how to utilize the need for luxury, elegance, and art which had been the patrimony of the ruling classes, but which could be rapidly extended to all the classes that aspire to prosperity and dominance.

Our dearest dream as artists and fighters has always been that of lifting the masses from their spiritual and material misery. If we had the opportunity tomorrow to remove their hunger, then their ignorance, then we could declare that we had achieved one of the fundamental objectives of our whole enterprise.

We can ask no better than that both the elites and representatives of the masses participate in the life of the collective, deciding on their own interests and their own destiny. The soviet (another scarecrow-word for every state's flabby bourgeoisie) is a reasonable and useful product of a new era, and is already so widespread in the form of unions, in administrative and industrial environments, that one wonders why it shouldn't be part of political and military life.

The officials who made war know very well how precious the words of ranked veterans can be to those in the trenches, or even the words of simple infantry, who see with marvelous clarity the dangers to come, the precautions to take, the modes and techniques of specific acts of war.

How many times have we had to remark that the precise and acute experience of the average soldier is worth more than all the syrupy treatises on the art of war concocted in Modena or Caserta?

In any case, why not admit these humble and acute representatives of the nameless masses to the direction of political, social, military, and administrative affairs, as advisers and interpreters of the majority's will? Naturally, all things being equal, this would involve no domination or dictatorship.

There is one thing I don't understand. Why can't this profound renewal be done on national and patriotic terms? In Russia, they defend the revolution, but also their territorial integrity, meaning their spiritual integrity. In Hungary, Germany, and Austria, the nation comes before everything else, and they won't hesitate to show their teeth to victorious nations that get carried away with annexation.

Only in Italy is Bolshevik socialism hermetically, ferociously anti-patriotic.

We might conclude that the Italian Bolsheviks have been bought by foreign money, and don't even have the basic prudence to maintain the facade. You want proof? Form some movement that is not useful to socialism, and is opposed to Italy, and you will be assured an alliance with the official socialists; vice-versa with Fiume. Does it harm the socialist cause? On the contrary, it benefits socialism. But since we are working for Italy, and not, let's say, Yugoslavia, they oppose us.

×　　　×　　　×

Once again: let's look to the east! Between Fiume and Moscow there is perhaps an ocean of shadows. But Fiume and Moscow are two luminous shores, and we must, as soon as possible, build a bridge between them.

INVITATION TO
THE DANCE

To the Ardent Youth of Italy

On the other shore they sleep the sleep of the just.

Sonorous, tumultuous, the massive waves of Fiumanism pass: religion and poetry of the new Italy, flown by the great wings of aircraft over the lethargic slumber of tired old Italy—in vain.

The vast, impassioned, castigating voice, pathetic and irate, magnificent and mordant, which animates our actions, the voice that all the dead of Italy's immense glory breathed through the throat of that complete and unique being, sings and admonishes in vain from the depths of Carnaro, flaking under the February sun like dazzling armor.

Is Italy sleeping such a deep and stupefied sleep that it cannot hear the loudest, newest, and most Italian voice that has spoken since Mazzini?[56]

---

[56] Giuseppe Mazzini was a politician who advocated for the unification of Italy.

×　　　×　　　×

After November 16th,[57] under the weight of the electoral victory that might be called the victory of multitudinous ineptitude, the youth of Italy, the same that won the war, gave no further sign of life. They even gave some signs of non-life: scholastic cramming, disinterest in political problems, absenteeism from every struggle, a tendency toward sterile polemics, egotistical couldn't-care-less attitude, restless pleasure-seeking, and social climbing.

This hurricane's high waves, which seemed ready to rise and break during the battle for votes, were instantly domesticated in a murmur of lagoon water, easily contained within those traditional embankments where all the ancient, putrefied trash is drained and rinsed.

The youth of Italy, after November 16th, was no longer ardent, proud, rebellious, or young. It was like the disillusioned performer, who retreats from public life after a few unhappy efforts and dedicates himself to the half-hearted enjoyment of his abortive glory, among the ever-present dupes fished from the wings of his last performance.

×　　　×　　　×

Have they returned to so-called serious studies? Are they back in their cowardly shell of preoccupation with career and employment? Have they fallen back into the filthy atmosphere of contests, titles, chairs, daily bread, and "great locations"?

Alas . . .

These things seem to have been buried by the war. The war

---

[57] This is a reference to the election of 1919, in which, as Carli points out, populism won over the Liberal Union.

gave a mighty kick to the filthy bourgeois mentality among young people "of good family," their spirit mortified by gradual injections of fear of the unknown and heroic adventure, made sterile by petty calculation, and limp with cretinous concerns.

Deplored for so many years, and just waiting to be swept aside by the rude broom of destiny, it's hard to understand how all this could survive the test of iron and fire on the flesh and souls of the soldiers.

How could these distinguished salamanders, who now want to "restore justice," pass through such a blaze for four years and not get burned? How can they now resume their studies, their business, their love affairs, their jobs, just where they left them, and with the same state of mind?

×   ×   ×

Positively "routine" mediocrity is the sign that struggle and greatness have been rejected. There is no greatness without irregularity, audacity, and madness. Lives destined for revolution and creation are made from those three elements.

The paunchy mollusks who defend the government in official and semi-official journals find that the Fiume enterprise consists precisely of irregularity, that the legionaries are all audacious and unscrupulous, and that the Commander is like a madman inspired by stupefying frenzies.

Youth of Italy, youth of Vittorio Veneto, can you see that triple definition without turning it upside down into supreme praise? I fear that your heads, bent over volumes that refuse to be absorbed as they once were; I fear that your backs, weakened by the shady indulgence of limitless pleasure; I fear that your minds, paralyzed by the avid calculation of income, subscribe with a grunt of distracted complicity to the miserable efforts at disqualification led by the toilet attendants who represent Cagoia's Italy. So, why is there no will, time, energy, or goodwill to join us in looking reality in the face? Why, to every claim to the inexhaustible idealism of our race, do you only ever manage to give the same response: "I fought in the war for four years. Now I need some rest, money, and pleasure. Leave me in peace."

×   ×   ×

We too spent four years at war, demobilized brothers. We too have the right to be tired and disappointed. We too would like to enjoy the satin and perfume of life, after so much steel and smoldering dust.

But we can't, we don't want to, and we don't even know how to. For us, the word "peace" has become an obsolete archaism, devoid of meaning.

We feel, with no distress, all the abysses dug by the war, between the past and us survivors, all the theories, traditions, and illusions it destroyed, all the new forces it hurled into the game of life to renew and inspire, to unleash energies and fantasies, and to offer new combinations, feelings, and situations.

There's no returning to the past. There's no returning to our old shape deformed by the cataclysm. We cannot wear the garments of bygone days. Nostalgia for the Arcadia of universal peace (which has never existed), for the idyll of tranquil speculations, serene study, uninterrupted pleasure, is now a utopia that should disappear from the heads of those who fought, like an unspeakable malady, unworthy of strong men.

×   ×   ×

Ardent youth of Italy, those of us camped out in Fiume, our obstinate love of Italy, our profound idealism, and our implacable need for struggle and spiritual adventure, now that we have the numbers needed for our action and unity, we are more decided than ever on not disarming our ideal fortress: Fiuman religion and poetry.

We don't need to be numerous. If quantity is almost always the opposite of beauty, it is still sometimes its corollary.

This is why we call you here—if not in person, then in spirit. Declare your Fiuman faith, defend it, rise up against those who offend it and want to destroy it.

Let me remind you of all the promises given and oaths taken during that delirious week of April 1919, in Rome, Milan, and anywhere else there were Arditi: the mass inscription of volunteers for Fiume and Dalmatia.

Where are all these promises and signed oaths now?

I repeat: we don't need numbers. But we need to let the veterans return home, and the infantry who gave many months to Fiume after four years of war.

So it wouldn't be bad if some of Italy's youth, those too young to have fought at Isonzo or Piave, could leave for the moment their desks of scholastic torment, their offices of slow stultification, the firms of fatal servility, and rush to the heat of Fiume, because Fiume is a gateway to mystery and miracle, laid open for not just the future of Italy, but above all the human spirit.

If it isn't entirely prostrate in the filth of Cagoia, or slumbering in obtuse egotism, the ardent youth will advance on this gateway.

And we'll initiate them with a brotherly hand.

THE FIRST STAGE
OF FIUMANISM:
THE LEAGUE OF FIUME

The First Light

The night when Gabriele D'Annunzio marched from Ronchi to Fiume was a "maternal" night.

It hid in its immense womb the largest and most powerful creation of the new era. It protected within its winged black cloak the most succulent fruit of four years of world war. It contained the essence of the martyrdom and passion of ten peoples baked together in a single nocturnal blaze, where the idea seemed subsumed by the individual, and where details were barely relevant, vanishing into the orchestral synthesis of the enormous All—the first new aurora after the chaos was created that night, the first renewing light after the perversity of satanic shadow.

The amazing little soldier, who emerged from one hundred battles mutilated but fierce, blinded but illuminated, felt and knew he was in some astral vibration, placing him at the head of a thousand rebels, at that moment so alone and simple and unarmed. He provoked the most tremendous of revolutions, announced the most divine of modern religions.

He was like one of those great portentous giants that blend into the night to fertilize it and give life to new divinities, to new worlds.

I groped around in the dark trying to trace his path. Then, I suddenly found it. His innate light illuminated the treacherous path: he was a magnet for the motors of the armored cars, a torch for the infantry, a headlight for the trucks: he was hope for all who followed.

Toward the Future

But how many saw that night the ideal contraband he was carrying under his lieutenant-colonel's beret? How many understood that the spirit was marching with him, that night, toward conquests even greater and more profound than that of a city that had given itself up?

The spirit was marching toward the future: simple as that.

The artist who had poured his tumultuous genius and the new modes of human eternity into dozens of books, the soldier who had thrown all his animating and destructive energy into the diabolical conflagration, the man who had lived every breath of his life like an intense lyric, wanted to give to the universal spirit, which soared above so much reaped glory, the new secret of the humanity that would have to be freed from its nocturnal casing by a miracle of knowledge and ardor, like a precious chrysalis from its intricate cocoon.

To give to the world the post-war formula: a form of thought more new than worn-out humanitarianism, more universal than nationalism, more idealistic than socialism, more heroic than communism.

We needed to console the victorious peoples, disappointed by the Wilsonian gaming of good faith, and the peoples humiliated by defeat.

Both had more than enough of commonplaces like *justice, civility*, and *liberty*, which provided cover for so much egotism and unspeakable rapacity.

Tired, disappointed, apathetic toward reconstruction and anxious about endless vendettas, these peoples rolled themselves up into snarling balls, tearing their own flesh, aching with neurotic rebellion against elusive tyrannies.

Gabriele D'Annunzio reached Fiume one September morning in a car, showered with flowers and smiles, as if for a feast of the resurrection for the people of Fiume.

How many really perceived what this car carried? Was the liberator of this sold-out city not also the builder of an Italy free of Giolittian Camorrism and bureaucratic professorship? Was he not the liberator of all those spirits enchained by dogma and prison-like traditions? Was he not the defender of all peoples who demanded to be the arbiters of their own destinies? Was he not the brotherly supporter of all heroism, the companion who reduced the suffering of the wretched? Finally, was he not the prodigious spirit who managed to associate the passionate love of one's country with the principle of universal brotherhood? From the courage of the Arditi, from the acumen of the builder, from the howl of the hungry proletariat, from the hatred of the anarchic destroyer, from the ecstasy of lyricism, from the gentility of the gentleman, from the perfume of the aesthete, he managed to compose a unique world, vigorous, manifold, full-throated, a superior world where there's oxygen for all, and from which all can obtain a generous helping of spiritual nutrition.

Realizations

Now, as he starts searching for the solution to the Fiume problem, with energy and political nous, the "realizations" begin.

Up until a few weeks ago, Fiumanism was one of those vague words that simultaneously mean many things and nothing at all.

Perhaps it was just the intonation, the style of the enterprise—the participation of the spirit, as the absolute ruler, in the action of men and weapons. For some it meant a religion, for others a philosophical or literary movement—in short, a tendency, non-threatening and poorly understood, pushed with difficulty by some aristocratic talents.

Instead, it is a real and genuine political movement (ideal, religious, and human all at once), which takes its name from Fiume, because the first act which initiated the movement was in Fiume and for Fiume: the rebellion of a small core of men, protected by a right and by a formidable heroism, who stood up to a powerful coalition of arrogant nations.

For those who understood it, this first revolt gave rise to the idea of combining in one compact fascio the disparate forces of all the oppressed of the earth—peoples, nations, social classes, individuals—to combat and defeat the overreaching, imperialistic bodies that aim to subdue individual and collective liberty, suffocate feeling and idealism, offend dignity, deflate all pride, to mock right, and to injure the keenest interests.

The League of Fiume

This fascio will be called the League of Fiume, a free and international association constituting Fiumanism's first real and tangible conquest.

Gabriele D'Annunzio will write the manual for this movement

of action and ideals. Meanwhile, I will try to indicate the general organizational outline.

All peoples, all nationalities, all individuals and groups of individuals, all parties and associations and religions that hold liberty and renewal as cornerstones, and that recognize it as personified in the gesture of Gabriele D'Annunzio, will send their representatives to Fiume, and will be part of the League.

Any delegates of a party that happens to inhabit a country governed by principles hostile to the League, but which stands in complete solidarity with the Fiume doctrine, will not be excluded from the League.

Thus the following peoples will send their representatives to the League: Fiume, the Island of Carnaro, Dalmatia, Albania, German Austria, Montenegro, Croatia, irredentist Germans, Catalans, Malta, Gibraltar, Ireland, the people of Islam (Morocco, Algeria, Tunisia, Egypt, Syria, Palestine, Mesopotamia, Persia, Afghanistan), India, Burma, China, Korea, the Philippines, Hawaii, Panama, Cuba, and Puerto Rico. The following oppressed races: Hebrews of various nationalities, the Chinese of California, the Negroes and Italians of America, and Armenians. The representatives of countries unjustly treated by the Conference of False Peace: Russia, Belgium, Portugal, Siam, Germany, Hungary, Bulgaria, and Turkey. And finally, the parties and groups sympathetic with Fiumanism, which exist already or will quickly form in Italy, France, England, and America.

It is clear that whatever action launches such a league will be infinitely more powerful and effective than the wreckage that is the League of (plutocratic) Nations.

Fluidity

It's the first stage.

And then?

We'll continue to advance. We'll broaden our horizons, deepen our human, vital activity. We'll attempt what has never been attempted. We'll hurl our intoxicated selves into the eddies of the unexplored. We are poets. Hurrah! But we are poets who want and know how to live, seekers of new formulae and occult substances. We've launched ourselves into this supreme adventure of the spirit, at the bottom of which we don't know what awaits us.

Meanwhile, go ahead and call us Bolsheviks. I believe that in our spirit, fitted with every comfort, there is room for Bolshevism. But please don't leave it at that. We do not want to be fixed up in one word, like a suit, our whole lives. Words, like suits, get worn out and torn up. Our fluidity changes form and color according to the terrible and imperious rhythm of thought. We don't want labels or barriers or fixed goals. The word of the future is the only one that fits, because only the future is unattainable and changeable and dynamic, while the past would only cause retreat, and the present would halt us.

Gabriele D'Annunzio is now called the comrade of Fiume's proletariat, as he was called the corporal of the Arditi, and the sergeant of the Bersaglieri.[58]

Don't be surprised: tomorrow he might take part in a rite with fakirs, or dance some "fantasia" with the most civilized Arabs of Egypt.

This is the privilege of genius, to cross into the thousand forms of creation, and it's his secret how he remains so immutably and miraculously himself.

---

[58] The Bersaglieri were at this time a troop of marksmen in the Italian army.

CAGOIA IN FIUME

Infiltration

More proof that cowardice and vulgarity spread more easily than courage and grace: The infiltration of Cagoiery, even in the mystical realm of Fiume, proceeds more rapidly than the spread of Fiumanism beyond Fiume.

The contagion of evil is always faster and more rampant than that of goodness. It's not that discord has arisen among legionaries united by the same idea and the same devotion to the luminary. There is simply an infiltration of "Cagoiery" (meaning: a spirit of surrender, pettiness, opportunism, profiteering, and fear) within the ranks of "Fiumanism" (meaning: a new spirit, heroic selflessness, foresight, and passionate love). A cloud of putrid gas, originating in the Roman sewers, has managed to descend upon the divine atmosphere of Fiume and has poisoned it. Hidden within the chlorotic cloud, some shady characters have joined us, made of baseness and deceit, and in good faith we trusted in their legionary uniforms, their false brotherly smiles, and their sacrilegious oaths.

Profiles

Cagoia walks the streets of Fiume, cleverly and generously clothed in legionary dignity and military decoration.

Anyone who passes with the absentminded gaze of the carefree follower, or absorbed by conscientious activity, will fail to recognize him. They'd have to recognize his famous image under a slew of new guises. But the more discerning observer, or the idle stroller who can pause for a moment, or those suspicious by instinct or by prejudice, will not struggle to recognize the Cagoian profile imprinted on a few hundred human faces, mingling with the faithful and expectant crowd of D'Annunzio's army.

Today, this treacherous chameleon prowls the streets in a carabiniere uniform. Tomorrow, more cautiously, he will be an infantryman or an Ardito, slightly altered but not too much, recognizable by the evasive gaze, the unsteady voice, and the hesitant and doubtful gait.

His business begins in a hotel room where the conspirators gather. He pauses in bars and cafés, lounges around the barracks, blends into rallies and assemblies, slips into head offices, skillfully slithers higher and higher, all the way up to the sacred places, right to the door of the great animator himself. Once there, he spies, listens, whispers, examines, probes, investigates, and searches.

He even obtains the trust of the leaders. He is given important duties, missions of trust, command of faithful troops, posts coveted by and sometimes denied to the truly faithful, who are too often left on the sidelines, unused or watched with suspicion.

Temperaments

I can spot Cagoia in any skin.

I could rip one by one all the insignia from all the cops who've been tossed among us, to mangle us with the weapon of hatred, to sew division within the unified soul of Fiume.

In the nudity of unveiled consciousness, you would see their mean little thoughts trotting along, the careerist preoccupations, the petty social climbing, the filthy, mercenary maneuvers. All the regurgitation of Roman money, all the rhythms of the most notorious political sewers can be so precisely identified in these vile mercenaries that you could draw up a dossier.

Cagoia is incarnated in everything that most resembles him in the ranks of the Italian army and police force: all that is impeccably carabiniere, retrograde, Jesuitically insidious, he sends to shatter the sacred compact of our organization of beauty.

Mentality

Naturally this importation of political filth belongs to the pedantic, scheming mentality of the old bureaucratic Italy.

We have all their names. We won't forget a single one. We'll publish them when the time comes. These wretches who've come to Fiume to provoke a civil war, these sell-outs, who want to undermine the holocaust and consign it bound and unarmed to Yugoslavia,[59] shouldn't be considered Italian.

They pretend to work in the name of a king of Italy who evidently cares nothing for Fiume and has no desire to hear its impassioned call, but in reality they do the work of the allies and

---

[59]"*L'Olocausto.*" D'Annunzio called Fiume a "*città olocausto*," "holocaust city," meaning a martyred city.

Yugoslavia.

They merit the utmost severity. If traitors and spies exist among us, there must be a court-martial. Fiume is currently at war with the universe. If we want our foreign enemies to genuinely fear us, we need to apply justice and give no room to dangerous indulgence, to our domestic enemies, merchants of defeatism immigrating from old Italy, long familiar with the classic defeatism of Giolitti and Nitti.

AMERICANISMS

Soldiers, do you remember when there was war, and we anxiously awaited our winter leave, and with the paper hardly a minute in our hands, we shone with mad joy, stuffed some things into our haversack, and headed by foot, by truck, or by train, toward home and love, toward warm rest and the cherished weeks of civilian life, where endless care and tenderness awaited?

And do you remember the fierce disappointment that our naive giving hearts experienced, setting foot in some station, walking some footpath or sitting in some café far from enemy grenades?

Disappointment in everything, all the time. The utter indifference toward our trench uniforms, of which we were supposed to be ashamed. The disgust with the mud running down our legs. The women who forgot "their" fighters or diverted themselves with draft dodgers. The mania for pleasure and profit, the ostentatious luxury. The attitude of pious protectiveness toward the veterans. The immense remoteness between spirit, body, and heart, between the nation and our youth, who were tormented and transfigured in the zone of fire and death.

Well, dear comrades, that same disappointment, that burning indignation, and that desire to escape from the cities to return immediately "up there" where there was love and heroism, where there was kindness and courage and true youth—I have felt it lately, peering into any city in Italy after a long period of delightful Fiuman exile.

Nausea, disgust, indignation. The need to rebel and swing a powerful club, smashing all and sundry. The urge to scream violently in the midst of a cravenly tranquil, elegant environment. An overwhelming desire to say, at every step, to every face, to every grimace: "Swine! Scum! Wretches!"

Indeed. Just as it was before, the indifference, arrogance, or hostility of those selfishly committed to their own business and pleasure, toward those who sacrifice themselves fighting for and defending something, are rife and ostentatious in their insolence.

As before, the layabout critics, eternal evaders of every struggle, and the comfortable, commonsense purveyors of intellectual mediocrity, yap their advice, deplore our "excesses," declare themselves "tired" (impotent cowards!) of the excessive extension of the struggle.

The soldier of Fiume, as the Italian soldier before him, is regarded as a bizarre animal, with which one doesn't and wouldn't want to have anything in common. He is approached with caution and suspicion, with a disapproving, contemptuous gaze that says, "who's forcing you!"

It's enough to pass Mattuglie to meet this rude moral chilliness square in the face. Carabinieri, customs officers, and functionaries are the first to make us violently aware of the hostile isolation in which the nation has left us. Censorship and the blockade—a marriage of convenience but also temperaments—makes us an inapproachable little island at the extremity of the vast ocean of indolence and national unconsciousness. At least it preserves us from the contagion of fatigue, and above all it preserves "the other shore" from the contagion of our spiritual beauty.

×   ×   ×

The train you board in Trieste takes you through that divine and terrifying zone where Italy, with its reddest blood, showed the whole world that it was a great and ardent nation.

The train glides slowly along, almost silently, across the domain of heroism and the thousand monuments to glory. The Carso, the Hermada, Montefalcone, the Isonzo—piles of untouched mesh fencing, long caverns, walkways, unexploded projectiles, flooded barracks, abandoned cemeteries.

Yes, but who is still looking out the window? Who is still interested in those recesses done in the Greek style, the lunettes, where the people of Italy built its future and its formidable grandeur?

In the dining car the steam of hot pasta emits a triumphant hymn, shamelessly steaming up the windows through which our memory had just been evoking other vapors, other sudden clouds: a surprise grenade, a bomb dropped from an airplane, a gas cloud; the symmetrical, trotting lights of the wagon obscure the fireflies of the second line barracks. Discussions about cost of living cause us to forget that perhaps here, or there, some hundred yards away, Giovanni Randaccio died,[60] or an assault unit rolled out, or a fighter plane took a fatal hit.

---

[60] Giovanni Randaccio was an Italian hero of World War I.

×   ×   ×

It's fine. The train is fast. Everything outside passes rapidly.

A more or less ministerial committee has been established which declared this place a "sacred area." Woe to him who takes the merest pin or splinter from this zone!

Sacred to the foreigners and tourists, it'll be the prettiest Museum of Italy, open to the Americans. "*Oh yes! Molto pellissimo!*"

Americanism! Americanism!

×   ×   ×

In Venice, there are American and British ships in the mild basin of San Marco: fighters and cruisers. They've been here from time immemorial. And they're not leaving. They haven't the slightest intention of ceasing to inconvenience us. And the inconvenience is huge and intolerable. The stars and stripes clash annoyingly with the beautiful bay's reflections, the marble and flowery loggias. And nobody really knows what these foreign boats are doing here. They serve only to remind us that we must hate, hate without limit all that is Nordic, all that is fair-haired, all that is not understood and does not understand us, all that is foreign.

But the good Venetian men and women do not share this opinion. All those with enough money to buy a new outfit every month, and the audacity to forget they're Italian, eagerly throw themselves into any lounge, like the Danieli, to entangle themselves with the blond sailors of John Bull or Uncle Tom for some jazz or foxtrot.[61]

They have such a delicate way of stepping on their partner's

---

[61] Since Carli pairs Uncle Tom (as opposed to Uncle Sam) with John Bull, the national personification of England, he is likely pulling a double entendre poking fun at America's racial problems.

feet! And such a charming manner of weaving their laughter, like orangutans thirsty for brandy, with the shrill little voices of Italy's amiable simpletons!

"You know that we women love to dance, and on the American cruisers they dance oh-so-sweetly to the rhythm of the lapping waves and the Anglo-Saxon bands. What a delight! Fiume? Ah, yes: there's also Fiume! But poor old Wilson, so maligned, at heart he's a true "gentleman"—so his officers tell us during an intoxicating dance, and keep the political phantasms at bay.

"Leave off with your Fiume and Fiumanism! Uncle Tom has it all sorted: peace and money. Italy will be happy because it has a great protector. Oh, if only we could be abducted to America!"

Dance, dance, little Venetian ladies, exquisite remnants of the 1700s, all rigged up and powdered! The Italy that so brutally beat its enemy didn't deserve your postwar languor.

You are worthy of your countess, who loved the studded and generously mustached Kaiser. And we who came to your defense at Piave! Ah! I understand now: you want nothing more than to be *invaded*!

LEGIONARY DYNAMISM

An easy criticism for superficial observers might be that for nine months we've *stopped* at Fiume, and that the enterprise of the nocturnal rebels of Ronchi is now a placid job of bureaucratic or military business.

Stopped. Immobile, static, inactive, settled, and organized, as if we were never going to leave. Right? And Fiume is also a delightful vacation spot, with enough light and sun and flowers to make the blue Riviera or the Sorrento coast jealous; girls with smiling eyes, and beautiful cafés full of delicacies, right? There's magnificent swimming in the Carnaro, there's no need for toil, and you can enjoy comfort and delight worthy of a Renaissance court, right? Every third day you see a parade or festival of flowers and imaginative words, which speak of new life and prodigious spirit, after which there are feasts seasoned with new enthusiasm and renewed Fiuman consciousness. Isn't that right, acidulous commentators of the cafés of every city in Italy?

The cruder conception of dynamism sees it as a "perpetual motion" up or down, east or west, perhaps even without aim or limit; in our case, a march toward any given objective.

But we move with more than just our feet, and it is not always marching legs that propel humanity forward. Most of the time, you walk infinitely farther while standing still, and asserting a new principle, imposing a pioneering idea, conquering a bastion of the future in one bold move. In other words, there are moral and intellectual advances that matter more than a long march toward an enemy province.

The apparent lack of movement from the legionary enterprise hides a dynamism that isn't plain for all to see, precisely because for nine months we never left the circumscribed confines of the holocaust, and we have forcibly compressed our activity between the parapet of Cantrida and the barrier of Sussak.

Moreover, simply remaining in Fiume—despite all the plots of the national government, despite the irregular character of the enterprise, despite the disruptive operations of the Zanellians and Italophobes,[62] despite the weaknesses, the betrayals, the desertions, and the thievery (all inevitable phenomena in any rebel enterprise)—by remaining in Fiume when we might well have been driven out by force or disbanded with cunning is to have completed many difficult steps toward the contested objective, is to have marched, marched, and inexorably marched.

And there are also hands. An army without unlimited funds or government aid, having to live day to day on subscription money and the meager supplies provided by patriotic charity, is forced to find for themselves the goods, provisions, sustenance, and

---

[62] Riccardo Zanella (1875–1959), leader of the Autonomist opposition to D'Annunzio. He would later become the only elected president of the Free State of Fiume, between October 1921 and March 1922.

comfort they need. This is where the daily exercise of audacity, skill, and organization comes in. It is a useful and wise way to employ combative energies, made for battle of every form, and incapable of simply waiting.

We legionaries had an undeniable stroke of luck in not being attacked by any real enemy. The capture of Nigra ended peacefully, or, to put it in legionary slang, "softly," because Nigra is Italian and couldn't be treated like a Serb or a Frenchman. All the arrests and subsequent escapes of legionaries from fortresses, remarkable in themselves, are, however, too isolated to constitute a mass phenomenon. The bulk of the Fiume army had no chance to engage in combat. It remained armed from September 12th onward, and if the Commander had not continuously injected it with hope and promises of a future offensive, it would have dissolved irreparably and lost all combat readiness.

It is precisely this constant work of exaltation and electrification, performed by the Commander and his best collaborators, that forms the foundation of Fiume's dynamism. The gradual development of an ideal program, maturing day by day; the seed of renewal and purification that the enterprise has carried with it from the very beginning: this is the true secret of its miraculous strength, balanced on the shaky stilts of the shady Cagoian war.

The spell of traditional discipline reinforced by war was broken by a handful of superior soldiers, who were the first to separate institutions from the homeland, and claimed the right to defend it against the government and military leaders. The revolutionary spirit of war was rekindled in a daring and fiery feat that still has no heirs. The right of all peoples and all races to choose their own constitution and form of government was proclaimed. All peoples who have rights to claim and chains of slavery to break were called upon and put in contact. The economic problem of the working masses was taken seriously, and a solution was imposed with a marvel of diplomatic wisdom and human psychology. The conditions of the local people were improved, and external rebellions against the enemies of Fiume and Italy were encouraged. This, in broad strokes, was the work of Fiumanism during these nine months of D'Annunzio's occupation.

We haven't been sleeping, as you can see. The progress is dynamic. We haven't left Fiume yet, except for the short trip to Sussak last May. Nevertheless, we've advanced. You might say we've been walking while standing still. We don't need much space. If we're still in Fiume, the ideas we've projected have now traveled far and wide—so far that no royal guard can catch them.

Fiumanism is a garden rich with capricious flowers that give themselves up to the most arcane pollen of the sea and mountain winds. This reddish pollen, born among the smiles of the beautiful coastal garden, carries the seed of revolt wherever it lands.

Have you never heard that a revolution can spring from a delicate garden of legend?

THE FUTURISM OF FIUME

When I'd just reached Fiume, I wrote to our friends in Rome: "Fiume is not a traditionalist city. It has only just recently emerged from an oppressive, authoritarian, and legitimist regime. It won't be long before we make it young again. The current atmosphere is decidedly Futurist."

And I was right.

You should see how this young and charming city rises spontaneously and unburdened from its ancient waters, helped by the recent audacity of Rizzo, Pellegrini, and D'Annunzio.[63] How ardent and anti-traditional its ways! Fiume is one of those cities destined to quickly forget its past and history, to head straight and unwavering toward a greater future. When the two-headed eagle had one head removed, there was a tricolor planted in its place.

---

[63] Luigi Rizzo was a very successful admiral in World War I.

The gesture is highly significant. It's the first sign that the city is beginning to shed its past and take on a new appearance and attitude.

It's enough to experience one day of festivities here to grasp the truly Futurist side of this mass movement. The fact that it's half-composed of women makes it more fresh and lyrical. It's a whirlwind of youth, of exuberant patriotism, which shouts, leaps, and whirls, and even drags in the few half-hearted or elderly ones who'd prefer to remain spectators.

I've never heard a packed square or theater sing with such violent intensity the hymn of the Arditi, which everyone here knows by heart. It's taken the place of the "Royal March" as the official anthem for all occasions.

I've never seen children of four or five years old (stubborn little things) congregate on front steps to give speeches beginning with "Children of Fiume! Kids of Italy! On this solemn day . . ." and closing with a momentous "hey, hey, hey! *Alala!*" All this happens in Fiume, because Fiume is a young city, spontaneous and assimilating.

FIUMAN ARABESQUES

A Long Pier and a Stomach Ache

This "ultimatum" of an afternoon led me to watch the mountain batteries moving to position. Colonel Rossi's gunners are wedged between white and crusted rocks that look like big sugar lumps. The test shots on the turbulent waters of the Carnaro are as invigorating as the fernet that I hurled into the convulsive folds of my agitated stomach.

The entire city of life seems to be suffering from an enormous stomach ache, and it responds with all the energy of its legionary youth. The muscular chains of the rusty anchors, like old, unused pitchforks, and the buoys resting on the ramparts of the pier, like monumental rubber rings for training the children of giants, all writhe and squeak as if suffering from indigestion.

The motorboats churning the all too calm waters of the port are like the first symptoms of some bubbling down below, set to prod the quays into convulsive motion.

The ships flash blue-gray with an aggressive sparkle. Every light is like the reflection of sharpening blades; every plume of smoke seems to rise from some murderous explosion.

Even the sun, funneled through a massive black cloud, hangs over the sea like the blinding fascio of some pitiless spotlight.

"War! War!"

And still, above us and in us, the atmosphere of heroism, the aggressive joy flickers in the gesture of the rowers, who cultivate the energy in their muscles like a limpid, well-kept weapon in its sheath. Are there still enemies to strike down? Or is it the delight of daring that keeps us armed and listening,[64] now that the earth no longer rumbles or pulsates with its ferocious convulsions?

Who knows? Disarming means—now and always—emasculation. And we insist on remaining masculine. Provided this isn't just some rusty old nightmare produced by the sour tomato sauce that covered our pasta.

I'd love to leap into the water, the animating spirit of vitality made drowsy from waiting. *Vroom*! But the powerful rhythm of the heart, rhyming with that of the elastic, pulsating sea against the dull rocks, is disrupted by the grim and malicious rhythm of my stomach, which a clawed hand squeezes like a helpless hand-kerchief in the hands of a washerwoman.

I remain nailed in cold and envious contemplation of the environment's dynamism, which flows toward me from all sides to make me its own.

Pale clouds, excited with curiosity, bend over the rectangular harbor, asking with voices of pubescent spring, "What will you do? What's going to happen?"

From the water, invisible *sipe*,[65] lobbed to net hauls of gullible

---

[64] "Daring" here is *ardimento*.

[65] A type of hand grenade used in both world wars, manufactured by the Società Italiana Prodotti Esplodenti.

fish, respond speedily: "We'll explode, my children; we'll explode. There's still so much steel to digest. It's given this coarse earth a horrible indigestion, thanks to your thunderstorms pregnant with metal, flushing all their waste down here!"

Yet the sea is still green, more Adriatic than ever. Everything enclosed within the islands seems like a track reserved for the exercise of our heroics, which await the night, more obliging than the Nittian carabinieri.

The skiffs and yawls are like light little dancers preparing for an evening in a slick and empty hall. There's an air of family everywhere. But the sun, stirring up the atmosphere now and then, gives the landscape the appearance of a house that—after the departure of a casket—has all its windows open to air the sheets.

It's the stomach ache gradually fading, unhurriedly, with murderous jolts, jolts that seem produced by the small floating mines of the blockade: plump toads full of poison, ready to splatter angrily on the majestic behind of the *Dante*, the well-fed, domineering whale who couldn't care less.[66]

As if by magic, a fresh quiver brings everything to sympathetic attention, all shiny and crackling brass. It's the Arditi fanfare, with the black flames advancing on the pier with D'Annunzio.

Youth: *sbrinn vasciololò!* The Commander sings as he marches; the stomach ache is sent packing. Fiume and I are energy once again.

The Hair of Spring

Naturally—after much searching—I found the formula for the Fiume spring.

---

[66] Carli is referring to the *Dante Alighieri*, the first Italian dreadnought battleship, which served as Italy's flagship in the First World War.

It's a spring that's in no hurry, a spring that waits. What for? The summer that kills it? Its god that deifies it? It doesn't matter. It waits and gazes upon the sea. All wonders, all liberations, arrive on the waters.

It was so eager to show itself in February, transforming the slender garden trees into umbrellas of light, fountains of color and laughter, rosy, violet, flesh-colored, white. It was more impudent than a precocious décolleté. It cheekily scolded the sweaty radiators and their damp, artificial atmospheres, and peeked out the double-pane windows that shivered in the winter sunsets of Monte Maggiore.

Then it disappeared in a gust of bora, which brought out the umbrellas, cleared the fountains, and extinguished all the laughter in a frigid drizzle.

Then it reappeared with rare splashes, lurking with surprises behind a wall, suddenly appearing among the Carsic rocks: *in no rush*.

Between one downpour and another, between the great sailing clouds of cotton, hurling gusts of swallows on the windowsills, filling the evenings already eager for criminal sensuality with guitars, it established itself among us with calm assurance, like someone on an important mission, but in no hurry to complete it.

×   ×   ×

But the Fiume spring also has another tendency. It is conciliatory, like an intelligent cocotte who wants to reconcile the contrasting characters of her various lovers.

One day, this incredibly generous female appears with the face of the Capri and Vesuvius spring: powerful and explosive like the gardens fermenting at the foot of the volcano, sumptuous like the hips of the wet nurses from Capodichino or the Ciociarian girls of

Anagni.

Another day she is soft, languid, and coquettish, like a Slavic girl from Zagreb, who descended on a raft along the Sava and came to spread her legs of lard and third-grade butter on the sands of Bùccari.

Yet another day she is rigid and austere, like a Hungarian merchant's wife, who barely conceals her warlike Magyarism under a fresh cosmopolitan skin.

Finally, she appears frenetic, mad, like a whirlwind, a petite Viennese blonde who loves her old waltzes, liqueurs, and nighttime excursions. A *political spring*. Perhaps inspired by the traditional, harmonizing wisdom of the emperor and king's governments. Today, she seems more like a traveling representative of the League of Nations, here to show the world that Fiume is an international city, living happily with its various characteristics and the balanced promiscuity of its races.

×   ×   ×

I know, just for us, my dear, an old crumbling wall from which a luxurious spring stream descends. It overflows from that wall like the hair of a radiant bacchante, an immense waterfall of wisteria and lilac, and a population of pullulating acacias. Every twilight, I go behind that wall, climb on a pile of friendly rocks, and fill my arms like a blind thief with the richest branches. I hold them in my arms as I would your tousled hair, and I run to you. Every twilight. And there is nothing sweeter than immersing your bright blonde hair in the dark, deep purple of that other spring hair.

Neutral Evening

Revolutions aren't made after lunch.

×   ×   ×

The aristocratic taste for disrupting ordered atmospheres and smashing the neat and normal arrangements of an overly static civilization clashes with the sentiment of the prudent masses, who believe in the religion of Order-Immobility, and fear the passage to disharmony necessary for the advent of more perfect harmonies.

But this aristocracy is in turn surpassed by a more refined sense of universal dynamism, in which the strong-willed creativity of genius overlaps with chaotic disorder, an end in itself for the anarchist.

Revolution for revolution's sake, like art for art's sake, is an intermediate stage, necessary to shake off quietism and weariness. But it would be criminal if it were not immediately followed by the creative phase, which turns the revolution into an instrument of human development.

×   ×   ×

Look at how the heroic potential of postprandial self-confidence, conceiving the most daring feats on the blood-red canvas of sunset while seated at a café table, sags and falls apart like the milkshake left to sit too long in the glass.

Music is a notable pretext, deserving the tribute of prolonged ecstasy. And beautiful women have every right to inject powerful narcotics into the already venomous hall, and awaken in hazy eyes the imaginings of a summer evening. Here the Arditi dagger gleams imposingly with ostentatious bravado that—oh, the spell of perfumes!—will never find an outlet. It will remain stuck in that grip, glimmering harmlessly, like a Kali Klor smile stuck in the teeth it adorns.[67]

It's good, madam, this Sangue di Morlacco, thick and sour like a ruddy kiss behind enemy lines. It's nice to drink this syrupy liqueur with slow dips of the tongue, looking the Ardito in the eyes, who belongs to his knife and his war cry, and which your disquieting, shaved beauty would like to nail down in this vile café chair.

Alas, Alas . . .

The mirrors concoct *je ne sais quois* conspiracies of cold lights that crystallize like multicolored *cassate* framed by geometric plates.[68]

The glasses distract with their rivalry of vain individualism, changing the color of their outfit just to get noticed: clowns vomiting their ephemeral souls, which they shed like a stage costume for the first adventitious master.

Bah! Outside is the firmament, which they say is severe. Should we go out? In Cantrida there are machine guns pointing down at us. Let's go see. What a pain, what a pain!

Revolutions, gentlemen, are not made after lunch.

×   ×   ×

The bitterness of these alternatives of realistic solidity and impalpable airiness is fueled every evening by malign explosions of electric light perched beneath stucco vaults, in corridors of mirrors that provoke limp reflexes and reflections of renunciation. We

---

[67] A brand of toothpaste, known for the beaming cartoon smiles in its advertisements.

[68] *Cassata* is a Sicilian dessert made with ricotta.

monitor our sensitive nerves, guilty of succumbing to the slightest environmental surprises, and prepare to despise ourselves with increasing irreversibility at each stage of our monstrous march, scattered from the ideal, ambushed by the seductive calls of April, bursting with scents too carnal.

The soul is more massacred by these pauses of suicidal neutrality than by a hundred blows received in the frenzy of battle, in a mad conflagration of all its chimerical beauty.

A NAME AND A
UNIFORM FOR COURAGE

When a people is engaged in a struggle that will decide its existence, success can hardly be expected if the people cannot find for this struggle a formula or a flag which expresses in total the inimitable genius of the race.

Each people makes war the way they know and the way they can. But it is condemned to defeat when it attempts to falsify its own fundamental characteristics, deforming its own mentality and instinct by trying to stereotype itself in formulae and flags that do not belong to it.

In the same way it threw the hatreds and antipathies of various bloodlines into the crucible, the great war which has just ended wanted these bloodlines to find their own specific modes and resources.

From the beginning it seemed that Germanism—which fell leaden and gloomy like an endless winter upon Latinity—would manage to impose its style of warfare: unrelenting collectivism, the drowning out of personality, bitter sacrifice with no glory, mass action enveloped in a deep and infinite gloom.

Since it was believed to the point of prejudice that combat should involve equal weaponry and equal styles, every army of the Entente tried to conform to this style of warfare, tried to create a German-style army, immense, compressed, elephantine, dark.

But our race could not and did not adapt to this pressure. The contrast between our aggressive, impulsive, individualistic, sensitive, rebellious character—and the kind of Nordic discipline that was being imposed—was too jarring. We would joyfully accomplish any given sacrifice for our Italy, at whose feet we generously laid our proud youth, but we didn't want our sacrifice to be obscure, useless, lost in the immensity of effort. We didn't want to be *driven* to death: we wanted to run to it of our own accord, with our dreamers' souls and impassioned hearts. We wanted to donate what was asked of us, donate all the most typical dispositions of our fiery southern nature.

For two and a half years we made war like Germans. We wasted away in the trenches, we tore our flesh on barbed wire, we let ourselves be automatized by the infinite repetition of monotonous daily duties. We resigned ourselves to forgetting our character. This is what the nation wanted, and we had to kneel. We were miraculously disciplined and obedient. But the effort that this compulsion cost us, the deformation it caused to our fundamental character—which could not simply wander off but had to suffocate in silence—provoked an inevitable reaction. All of our genuine, compressed and tormented energy, from the depths of our individuality, screamed in anguish and called for liberation.

If this cry of agony had been heeded, and remedy had been sought straight away, not only would the Caporetto misadventure have been avoided, but the war would have been won perhaps a year earlier. The worst fault that men can be accused of is that of not understanding each other. The absence of psychological acumen — that is, knowledge of human values — is always the first cause of all drama. In war it leads to disaster.

And we did not understand each other. The youth of Italy was hurled into the trenches without a thought for how to valorize its most distinctive qualities, its unbridled audacity, to bring its cheerful vigor to the surface, to discover and exploit its acrobatic potential, its adventurous and breakneck initiative. Instead, they were shaped into an enormous gray multitude, uniform and dolorous. Here and there, anonymous flames and sparks would escape, astonishing the world. But they were *anonymous*. This was the problem. Why not give them a name?

The Italian soul groaned, chained and condemned to create flashes of stupendous beauty without anyone managing to locate its source and consecrate its glory. Leaning into Germanic collectivism: what a terrible mistake!

×　　　×　　　×

How many times, witnessing some stupefying feat achieved by one of our own, by some humble infantryman, a mere number, have we exclaimed: "But this beats the audacity and beauty of any hero of antiquity! This one needs to ascend the ranks, be a leader, a guiding light!"

But who ever spoke of him? Who ever heard about him? Who gave him the post he deserved? His glory, alas, never went beyond his company, or occasionally his battalion. Perhaps he received a dozen lines in the official awards bulletin, and all talk of him stopped there.

On the peaks of our martyrdom, marching single file for those fabled mule drivers, bent under the weight of a *cheval de frise* or trellis, exhausted, sweaty, tattered and filthy, our studded boots submerged in the mud, how many times did we freely cast off our load to rush to danger, bare and disheveled, a blade between the teeth and a grenade in our fist?

How many times, in our so-called "rest" periods, worn out and weakened by a long march with packed satchel, cartridge boxes, rifles and haversacks, did we anxiously anticipate some encounter with the enemy, some alarm to galvanize us, some whiff of conflict that would allow us to drop the weight that united our shoulders with those of the mules?

I first saw the Flames at the Sella di Dol, on San Gabriele, one night in September 1917.

Up to that point I only had a vague notion, which had filtered through the ranks like a beautiful and mysterious legend. The troops never wondered at this prodigious phenomenon emerging from their own company, like the flight of a young eagle abandoning its dull and static rock. After all, each soldier felt within himself the possibility of becoming, under certain conditions, an Ardito. For example, there were certain elders who would typically straggle or remain idle for whole days in the trenches. But as soon as one of the younger troopers (born in '97 or '98) stung them with some motto, taunt, or sarcasm, they'd snap and grab their rifle, swing it like a club, and assail the first in reach, shouting in their face:

"I'm stronger and more *ardito* than you—when I want to be—longhair!"

The key to their psychology was in this "when I want to be."

It meant: "Take away my satchel, a pinch of discipline (just a pinch), don't wear me out with overly long marches, don't leave me too long in the trench, give me better food, a bit more money, some distinction that tells everyone I'm brave, praise me before the company, give me responsibility and a little pride: and you'll see that no Austrian will scare me. I'll refuse no patrol, no incursion, no advance. Let me be *Italian*, and I'll be Ardito."

This is what our soldiers believed and felt. Not just the few who rushed to form the first assault units, but all or almost all of them, young and old, veterans and barely initiated recruits, as well as those who decided not to leave their old regiment.

You want to know why? Our soldiers have never feared combat. The words "going to the front," so dark and foreboding, were much less a nightmare due to the blood, flames and peril, than the infernal fatigue, the indescribable discomfort, the mortal tiredness, the inextricable mesh of ills and pains that awaited them.

They were ten times more willing to give their own life, if they could give it *better*, if they could *be themselves*, if they could fight with agility and liberty, as Italians.[69]

Italy lacked precisely the concrete formula to channel the beauty and superior audacity of its heroic youth, scattered to the wind and left undiscovered. *It lacked a name and a uniform for courage*. It needed to gather up and make distinctive the one hundred thousand hidden potentialities that were suffocating under a buttoned-up jacket. The jacket was opened, and the valiant heart opened with it. The youth of Italy beamed with joy. Their eyes shone with exceptional possibilities; their hands reached for their daggers.

And that miraculous synthesis of our race, the Ardito, leaped out.

The Ardito, the futurist of war, the unkempt vanguard, ready for anything, light and agile, unbridled, the cheerful force of twenty-year-olds throwing bombs while whistling showtunes. We finally discovered a type of soldier that was *ours*, absolutely ours, distinct from the bersagliere, the alpino, the French zouave,

---

[69] Italianamente ("Italianly")

the German patrolman, the Austrian assault trooper, and adapted to the most extravagant undertakings and the most incredible risks, to adventures that reach the fantastic and the legendary.

The essential character of our people was finally recognized and unleashed: agility and physical courage, guided by personal initiative, and inspired by the highest idealism.

The existence of a youth that was new and instinctive, free and unprejudiced, healthy and gifted, a youth that wanted to transcend, overflow and anticipate, finally made itself heard.

The vanguard of a nation at war had been created.

A CHIVALROUS DISPUTE BETWEEN THE ARDITO MARIO CARLI AND THE CARABINIERE CABRUNA

From La Testa di Ferro, *May 23rd, 1920.* [70]

Following comments we published in Issue 15 of our paper regarding the Cantrida incident, Lieutenant Airman Ernesto Cabruna of the Carabinieri Corps, holding himself a champion of their honor, which he considered offended, published a statement in the *Vedetta d'Italia*. In this statement, he declared that he returns in kind the spittle that those responsible for *La Testa di Ferro* had aimed at the Royal Carabinieri who so ignominiously fled.

He accused them of having meanly struck even the dead, and invited them to an exchange of bullets. Our director, Captain of the Arditi Mario Carli, sent his representatives, Major Giuseppe Nunziante of the Arditi, and Second Lieutenant Germano Pellizzari of the grenadiers, the first wounded in Cantrida, to offer

[70] *La Testa di Ferro* (*The Head of Iron*) was a journal created by the Futurist fascio of Fiume (the *Fascio Futurista Fiumanese*), which included Carli, Guido Keller, and Mino Somenzi.

Lieutenant Cabruna the satisfaction he had requested. The same was done by Second Lieutenant Cesare Cerati through lieutenants Marcelli and Rossi. Another of our editors who had written articles on the Cantrida incident, the volunteer Forti, being unable to send his representatives to Lieutenant Cabruna due to the difference in rank between them and not wanting others to answer for what he had written, made it known in a letter to Cabruna that he was the author of part of the writings in question, reaffirmed them, and assumed full responsibility.

His letter remained unanswered. Regarding Cerati, the representatives of both parties, after meeting, acknowledged that there should be no reparation through dueling, excepting the rule that more than one person from a community can go to the field for offenses committed or received by that community.

It was thus established that only Captain Carli would duel with Lieutenant Cabruna. The encounter took place last Tuesday, with Lieutenant Ceccherini serving as the second. The two opponents exchanged four shots with pistols at a distance of eighteen paces, using the same weapon, so that one offered himself unarmed to the shots of the other.

Lieutenant Cabruna, favored by luck, fired first. On the fourth shot, Captain Carli hit his opponent in the side, and the wound was recognized as sufficient to prevent the continuation of the duel, which thus came to an end. Since Captain Carli had not directed any personal offense toward Lieutenant Cabruna, and he had no intention of retracting what he had written about the other carabinieri of Fiume in any way, there was no reconciliation.

WE ARDITI

The Cradle of the Arditi

I saw them for the first time in 1917, on San Gabriele. Flashes on their lapels; jackets open; sweaters with skulls; pockets full of grenades, sharpened daggers; muscular, brutal little bodies; black and resolved eyes; not many words.

To we who lay like animals in a den of mud and rock, in a dominated position where you could hardly use a pick without drawing a tempest of gunfire, that army of unbridled demons, proud and intrepid, who had just attacked the cowardly enemy in their insidious, labyrinthine hideout, was like a sudden gust of liberation. It was our spiritual emancipation that we saw in them: a rediscovery of ourselves and our most profound virtues, the expression of our most sincere style, the realization of our most irresistible aspirations.

Their assault was quick, sudden, and silent. No artillery fire, no alarms. After a rapid exchange of whispered orders, like a densely packed group of conspirators, each moved toward his goal. They crawled, jumped, and struck with such lightning speed that not even the victim's cry was heard. Then, in the palest night, sleepless, feverish, facing the caverns of the "Fort" where infernal resistance had nested, the monstrous flamethrowers flashed. Perfidious, incandescent serpents reached the enemy in their deepest recesses, leaving them incapable of using their weapons.

The precision, stealth, and confidence with which the Arditi attack was conducted gave it a miraculous quality. None lagged behind. The commander (a real daredevil) leading the way could advance with peace of mind, because his men were all following him like some infallible mechanism in which each part was assigned its own particular battle sector, its own Austrian to strike down.

And their action was always a success, to the point of perfection.

×　　　×　　　×

But the Arditi had their precursors. I don't mean the Roman light infantry, the Velites, nor the battle of Legnano's Company of Death, against which Barbarossa broke his grotesque Nordic claws. No, those are too distant and different from us.

In the war that is just over, a year before the Flames were created, there was an official of Garibaldian spirit, with real guts and personal charm as well as a great sense of psychology: Captain Baseggio. As the enemy came hopping from mountain to mountain towards the gorgeous plain of Vicentino, as our regiments rushed to fight off the breaking tide, Baseggio organized a separate force of volunteers who would mercilessly prick and inflame the enemy's flanks. The motley band of men recruited for this guerrilla warfare, of every age and specialty, was given the name "Scout Company of Death."

Little formal discipline, no bureaucracy, sketchy hierarchy, a squad of officers might be commanded by a soldier, as long as he was astute and *ardito*. The group was united only by the personal charm of the commander, and individual honor, pride in success, thirst for glory, and above all love of one's country, which stood in for any sense of duty. Besides the unbridled desire for liberty, these men had an enormous disdain for the enemy as well as for their own life. They had a need to fight of their own accord, without restriction or permission. The only prize they aspired to was the "bravo!" of Baseggio, and, if they survived, three days' leave to go drink a liter of Valpolicella at the hearth of some nice *tosa*.[71] But they'd all be present for their next appointment.

They knew their absence would not be condemned at any war tribunal, yet they always returned.

"Ready, captain! Where are we going?"

How Italian it all is!

The Austrians knew by heart the legendary captain's name, and when they heard his call in the trenches they trembled and fled, those most disciplined of soldiers of an iron empire.

×   ×   ×

Meanwhile, wanting to award and distinguish the bravest from the masses, those who tackled the patrols and surprise attacks, every regiment, each of which already had its own "Scouts" and "Wire Cutters," established cores of soldiers who were baptized the "Arditi" due to their distinguished acts of warfare. They were given an insignia to wear on their jacket sleeves: a V and an E crossed and underlined with a Savoy knot.

This was the first timid step toward our military's inevitable

---

[71] Venetian word for "young woman"

revolution.

The tendency, above all, was to clearly separate the fighting masses into two categories: those who had an aptitude for attack, and those who were better at resistance. On one side, the youngest, the carefree, the unkempt, the unscrupulous, the restless, the violent, the discontented, the champions, the passionate, the frenetic, the unbridled, the gymnastic, the sportsmen, the mystics, the jokers, the vanguard of every aspect of life, the futurists of the head or the heart or the muscles. And on the other side, the elders, the family men, the slow, the heavy, the passive, the disillusioned, the idle, even if for the most part good soldiers, but more inclined toward obedience than initiative, more stuck in their ways than impatient to take off, pillars in the trenches but hardly ideal for pushing forward.

The first generally came from the cities, the rest more often from the country.

These Arditi of the regiments were established according to a criterion of distribution determined by the war effort. They did not, in fact, act as lookouts in the trenches, but rather remained in reserve with the battalion or regiment command, never received any extra pay or better rations, and were deployed for patrols and capturing advanced enemy positions. They weren't assault troops in the true sense of the term.

×   ×   ×

But the strange and suggestive name "Arditi" was already familiar throughout the army. All of a sudden, it seemed a new type of soldier had been discovered, whose moral prerogatives were suggested by the name. For the first time, a corps was baptized not according to its specific methods of warfare (grenadiers, *bersaglieri*, bombardiers, etc.), but according to the singular values of its elements. For the first time, courage replaced the crest, the flame of love took the place of the flash, and genuine character carried the honor of an official title.

The definitive establishment of the assault units is due to the audacious and modern genius of one general. Besides being a rare man of war, he was an acute psychologist, with a mind capable of swiftly absorbing general ideas. His name was Luigi Capello.

It was he who intuited the very special role that could be filled by these slightly irregular troops, the decisive function that would be entrusted to these men who were fresh and fit for battle, rather than stultified by long stints in the trenches.

General Capello, then commander of the 2nd army corps, that magnificent corps that had covered itself in glory at Bainsizza, Santo and San Gabriele (glory that no Caporetto would ever cancel), and to which I am proud to have belonged, created the first two assault units in the spring of 1917 with elements from various regiments.

The first headquarters was at Subida, near Cormons. The general entrusted its creation to General Grazioli, division commander at the time, who would become commander of the *corpo d'armata d'assalto* on the Piave a year later.

Command of the two battalions was assumed by Colonel Bassi, who became famous among the Arditi for his strong character as a soldier and leader.

Few understood the deep significance and true character of the Arditi as General Capello and Colonel Bassi, the originator and the first instructor of our glorious corps.

"Arditi-style" training began in the minuscule camp in Subida. This training was later adopted by all the assault units, and aroused the admiration and wonder of all who witnessed it, not least the king of Italy, General Cadorna as well as various foreign missions.

After the May operation, there were six assault units with one thousand men each. Since the Subida camp was no longer large enough, they were transferred to Sdricca di Manzano on the Natisone river.

Above all, their exercises had the character of *war gymnastics*. They were trained by a gymnast of practical, modern views, Captain Racchi, who had discovered a variety of ingenious methods to prepare the soldier for combat without boring him with long theoretical instruction.

He popularized certain forms of jiu-jitsu which best suited the Arditi style of warfare. He trained them in melee combat in the following manner: one soldier held a rifle horizontally, gripping tightly with both hands, while another soldier would try to snatch the rifle away. The struggle would descend into frenzy until a sudden "halt!" from the instructor would force them to stop immediately and stand to attention. Disciplined violence.

Then there was knife combat. Each man would have something in front of him to strike: a ball of hay or an upright sack of rags. Each man would hurl himself at the target with his knife. At times the heat and ardor were so intense that the man's eyes would fill with blood and he'd end up seeing the unfortunate target as a genuine enemy.

A curious lesson in courage, which recalled the legend of William Tell, involved placing a soldier at attention as the instructor launched a lead pendulum to knock off the soldier's cap. Those who could watch the metal mass rush toward them and manage to stay still were judged exceptionally brave.

Even jumping had a specific modality of war. You did not jump a tightened cord or half-meter ditch, but rather a bundle of barbed wire.

The training for assaults, which was introduced for all units, was extremely dangerous and interesting: a true school of courage.

It involved storming a hill that was fortified and defended by barbed wire, trenches, caverns, walkways, and machine gun nests. Behind the Arditi there were machine gunners and small cannons. These would barrage the first line of trenches, as the Arditi advanced and lobbed their grenades. When they reach the trenches, the artillery starts firing at the second line. After the briefest of breaks, the Arditi resume their attack, *right under the firing arc of the artillery*, for another two or three lines.

The training was dangerous, I can't deny it. But it forged heroes. The fictional battle differed so little from the real battle — there were so many affinities in terms of emotion and risk — that when it came time to meet the Austrian, his presence was barely noticed.

There were injuries during training, and even some casualties, but these were due more to the excessive ardor of the soldiers than to any problem with the training. In any case, nobody was particularly shocked by these occurrences, since they were almost "the style" and to be expected.

Troops from across the whole army, officers from other army corps, as well as allied officers came to witness training in the Sdricca camp. They were all united in their admiration. Colonel Pavone, commander of the Arditi of the 3rd army corps, visited Sdricca many times and profited immensely from this model.

In the August operation on Santo and Bainsizza, the assault units were deployed in large numbers for the first time. From the outset, what distinguished them was the violence of their attack, which became a form of self-defense.

The Austro-Hungarian officials who were captured during the attack expressed great and spontaneous admiration for the Arditi, who they called "diabolical" (Teufelmenschen): "they came from every direction, crawling from wherever they were least expected, leaping from where no one would have imagined them, dagger between the teeth—grenade in hand—blazing eyes—imperious orders to put your hands in the air" (Bulletin of the 2nd Army Corps Command no. 2184, August 29th, 1917).

Between the Bainsizza offensive and Caporetto the Arditi continued their training at Sdricca, from where they would occasionally be detached and sent to Kal or San Gabriele to consolidate some recent conquest. The operations in quadrants 800 and 814 and Fortino, of which I was an impatient spectator, so splendid in their speed and overpowering victory, demonstrated how much force there was in troops who hadn't been drained by the torment of the trenches.

The Arditi of the 2nd army corps—precisely that army corps which they had tried to defame—always departed not with the calm resignation of someone fulfilling a duty, not with the forced smile of someone trying to maintain some dignity, but rather with an explosion of barbaric joy more suited to a carnivalesque orgy than imminent battle. It was an outbreak of music, song, and half-negro dance, with *putipù*, *scetavajasse* and *triccheballacche*, whose echo, if it had reached our stinking trenches, would have had us believe that the draft dodgers behind us were having some fun.

And they were indeed enjoying themselves, those spirited flames. Every time they were called to battle, the valley would overflow with their youth and enthusiasm. They left in trucks, in clouds of dust and exultation, saluting the company and swearing on the point of their daggers that they'd win.

And they always won. Not once did they return disappointed. Not once did the shadow of failure touch their proud black devil faces. Of course, some soldiers didn't come back, but they were very few, and they were always avenged. For one dead Ardito, at least twenty Austrians would have to pay the price.

They were never prisoners, nor did they take any. Getting

caught by those dogs? It meant shame and death among the wretched. Better to escape with a dagger in the belly. And as for capturing others and bringing them back? Useless ballast, costly and dangerous. No way! End of discussion.

Amid such heroism, such enthusiasm, such national pride, how could anyone suspect an imminent disaster? There wasn't the slightest clue here, no presentiment, no cause for alarm. One day, however, a solitary shout was heard in that spirited atmosphere. After a training session viewed by a few Alpini companies, over the din of Arditi hurrahs hurled into the clear September sky, an Alpino cried, or rather slurred: "hurrah for peace, *dio boia*."

Was it some kind of symptom? A watchword? A cry of the soul? A snippet of some papal encyclical? The Arditi didn't get it. Their souls were conditioned by battle and patriotism.

After witnessing the enemy invasion run rampant, trembling with rage and sorrow, had they been permitted to launch a timely counteroffensive against the enemy flanks with other brave companies, perhaps they might have averted Caporetto.

The Aristocracy of the Arditi

Since the synthesis of Italian valor was personified in the last two great battles of June and October, by the open jackets and flashes, everyone is now interested in the Arditi. Everyone talks about them. Everyone wants to pass judgment or pose questions. But how many really know what the Arditi are, their value, what they have done and will do? Very few, and even those are ill-informed. In Italy, people are very often ill-informed on issues of capital importance.

So it's not surprising that two contrary views, both divergent from reality, have been formed about us.

There are those who speak of the Arditi as legendary warriors:

mysterious people, beyond the law, thirsty for slaughter, whom it would be ill-advised to approach. Bloodthirsty, knife-wielding assassins, dagger between the teeth, provocation, thuggery, ferocity, the brutality of an orangutan. Blood for blood's sake, art for art's sake. Professionals of war, they'll be cutting throats, eviscerating and stabbing as long as they live. The most dangerous of beings, who want nothing to do with peace or civility.

The other view, in reaction, tries to depict them as the most ordinary men, who simply have better organization and more *esprit de corps* than the other troops. Prezzolini, in a *Popolo d'Italia* article, wanted us to face the incomplete and Germanified physiognomy of our assault troops. According to him, the new Arditi, those of the assault divisions, were the perfect expression of this type of soldier, to which he does not grant a monopoly on courage or individual initiative, but only increased discipline, more physical endowments, more instruction, more cohesive force. He goes so far as to place them with the *Sturmtruppen* of the defunct Austro-Hungarian army.

Without hesitation, I can say that the first view is in complete bad faith, while the second is the product of myopia and a lack of psychological insight.

There are those who have reason to fear and frown upon the Arditi's return home. Those who enriched themselves during the war, those who hid away or grew fat, those who were traitors and deserters, all conspired in some way for defeat, and all know that in the returning Arditi they will find inexorable avengers. Those who try, via fraud or flattery, to seize the advantages of peace, exploit victory to their own ends or neutralize the results; those who try to distract public attention from the problem which must come before all others, *the spiritual and material grandeur of Italy*, know all too well that the Arditi, bodyguards of the victorious nation, will use any means to block their efforts.

This is why the local Leninists, the bourgeois quietists and the conservatives who conserve only their paunch try to discredit those who over the last year brought the most energy to the war. This is why certain ladies and old fogies—those with no fiancé or son in the Arditi—cry bloody murder that we are mostly thugs flushed from prisons, or future convicts. After all, we carry daggers, don't we?

Those who claim that the Arditi are nothing but a "select and disciplined troop," without the idealism, the lyricism, the personality, and the character which is their true power and their purest glory, are equally wrong. They deceive themselves in good faith, and in good faith they deceive those who listen to them. Because yes, on occasion, their distorted chatter manages to devalue us, to dampen the enthusiasm of the nation that only vaguely recognizes our value, to de-idealize us.

×   ×   ×

As an Arditi official of clear mind I feel I have the right to offer a judgment of my comrades in arms, who I have known in the thousands and seen in all contexts: in combat, in training, on the march, in cities.

There is no greater, more complete or intoxicating pride for a fighting Italian than to be an Ardito. There is no glory of ingenuity or creation equal to that of having attacked the Austrians with knives and grenades. There is no courage comparable to that of sneaking into a machine gun nest with one or two comrades and sowing terror with a flamethrower.

There is in fact a hierarchy of courage. There isn't just one kind of courage. The Arditi occupy the highest point of this hierarchy. *The courage of the Arditi is not like all the others.* It might seem paradoxical, but that's how it is. It's a case of selection, an essentially *aristocratic* phenomenon.

×   ×   ×

Voluntarism. Disdain for the daily grind, where nothing is risked and not much is gained. Desire for emotion, for danger, for struggle. Personality, initiative, fantasy, the shrewdness of a predatory animal. A spirit of adventure, and *esprit de corps*. Gasconism of the deed, more than the word. Romanticism of the blackest foundation, on which gleams the musculature of an acrobat. Intellect founded in glory, generosity that reaches a refined aesthetic. The arrogance of knowing one's value. The perfect fusion of thought-beauty-action. The elegance of a primitive, child-like gesture following a gesture of unbelievable heroism. All the drive and violence with which the Italian soul overflows.

Aristocracy of character, muscle, faith, courage, blood, mind. Nobles dismounting their horses, aviators descending from their planes, intellectuals exiting ideology, refined fugitives of salons, mystics nauseated by the church, students hungry for life, and youth, youth, youth that will conquer all or lose all, that will give, in all its fullness, health and energy, its nineteen years of love for Italy, for all the beautiful things of Italy, the beautiful women of Italy, the future of Italy.

These are the Arditi of the Piave, of Montello, of Solarolo, of Asolone, of Pertica, of Valbella, of Monte Corno. These are the terrible assassins that the hags and fogies and Bolsheviks fear.

Assassins, yes. But it's only the enemy they kill, and traitors and renegades.

Doff your caps, gentlemen, for anyone who fears them must be an enemy of Italy.

1918, a Year of War

I have said elsewhere that the greatest war effort in 1918 came from the Arditi.

The heaviest burden, and without doubt the greatest offensive power: this is what decides the real energy of an army, by which all sorts of losses can be surmounted, with which operations are resolved and concluded.

The bulletins of our high command speak repeatedly of operations performed by the assault units in late winter and spring. In January, the 20th at the Col del Rosso and the 22nd at M. Valbella; in March, the 8th at Cavazuccherina, the 10th at Val Posina; in April, the 13th at M. Melaghetto; in May, the 13th again at Stoccaredo; and others in June on the Piave, in the days before the futile Austrian offensive.

The account given by high command of the battle in June, while giving ample attention to the resistance of brave infantry, credits the assault units with the most responsibility for counterattacks and recapturing positions.

The 52nd, on the Col del Rosso, fought a bitter battle to successfully retake the Costalunga redoubt.

The promontory of Solaroli was retaken with repeated attacks between June 16th and 24th by the 18th unit, which lost its best officers and the most epic of Arditi.

On Montello, the 27th unit worked with the armored cars in the Giavera counteroffensive, and joined the bersaglieri to attack the enemy between the Piave and Casa Carpanedo, forcing them back and taking prisoners, The next day (day 16) they returned to attack with infantry.

The 1st assault division, formed around the same time, was active on the Piave, more precisely in the vicinity of Fossalta, Fossetta, Croce, Zenson (June 17th–19th).

Also mentioned are the 11th, 23rd, 25th and 26th units, distinguished by their ardor and spirit of sacrifice.

But if we were to cite just one example of *ardimento*, it would be the 9th unit commanded by the intrepid Major Messe, which accomplished prodigious acts of valor in the Grappa region.

On days fifteen and sixteen, the enemy had managed to overwhelm the defenses of Col Moschin, Fenilon, and Fagheron, and occupy Palazzo Negri, Casa dei Pastori, and Cà dei Briganti. The unit receives the order to go to Col del Gallo before proceeding to recapture the Col Moschin-Col Fagheron line. It is December 15th when the Flames, marching rapidly, reach the position they needed to capture.

The operation begins with one company launching a decisive attack on Palazzo Negri, Casa dei Pastori, and Cà dei Briganti.

The fighting is especially ferocious due to the Austrians' reliance on machine guns, which chant their constant *de profundis*. But in less than half an hour, with bombs and daggers, our soldiers manage to dislodge the enemy and launch an attack on quadrant 1318, which has just been captured.

During the operation, Captain Umberto Pinca dies bravely leading the unit. His soldiers all swear on his body to avenge him. Meanwhile, a second column arriving from Fagheron drives out the Austrians occupying the church of San Giovanni, and clears the nearby woods.

Enemy units try to mount some resistance from the forest caves, but their defenses are quickly destroyed with flamethrowers.

The victors collect a good number of prisoners as well as five machine guns, and then take quadrant 1318 Fagheron-Col Piazzoli line.

Patrols that had pushed on to Fenilon and Col Moschin inform command that the two positions are heavily fortified.

Attacking Fenilon, the Flames, covered by artillery, roll down from quadrant 1318 and close in on the enemy position.

At 2200 hours the unit begins attacking with overwhelming force. Rushing on Fenilon, they surround it in a vice grip of grenades and flamethrowers. The smoke is so thick that not even the flamethrowers illuminate the fighting. The enemy put up a good fight in their desperation, but the Arditi are an all-consuming fire.

There is no escape. Those who don't surrender are killed on the spot. Our men cry the name of their leader, "Messe, Messe." When one Flame is killed, ten rush to avenge him. A magnificent battle takes place on Col Fenilon, where the Arditi had decided to baptize the banner of the ladies of Potenza. The inferno lasts an hour, after which the Arditi have total control, and Fenilon is back in our possession. The loss of five officers and more than one hundred soldiers, as well as the number of captured machine guns, testifies to the tragic nature of the clash.

During the night, the Arditi receive the order to proceed to the saddle of Col Moschin to launch their attack.

At seven, everything is ready. As our artillery begins to fire, the Flames, who nobody can hold back, rush to attack with a quivering, indescribable enthusiasm that had taken hold of everyone.

The Flames take it upon themselves to hunt down the Austrian the same way an animal is hunted in the forest—he is flushed out, baited, rattled and trapped.

Nothing can stop them; neither the hailstorm of projectiles nor the machine guns firing on their flanks. Again, anyone who doesn't surrender is killed on the spot. "Hurry up!" a small, jumpy Sardinian cries, his voice somehow carrying across the whole battlefield. The daggers have lost some of their glimmer, but they're cutting with greater force, as if in a rush, and the characteristic, piercing bursts of the bombs merge into one great tumultuous and terrifying fury.

Ten minutes after the attack signal, the Arditi have secured the plain. We still have twenty-seven officers, four hundred troopers, seventeen machine guns, and one trench cannon, plus two batteries with full munitions, and all kinds of precious material.

After the unit is replaced on Col Moschin and they return to the rear of quadrant 1318, the captured artillery fire blank rounds to honor the tireless black Flames.

On that same prodigious day, His Excellency Commander of the Grappa Division, General Giardino, sent out the following phonogram to all the other divisions: "With a marvelous push, the 9th assault unit retook Col Moschin in ten minutes, capturing more than four hundred prisoners, as well as twenty-five officers, and a great number of machine guns."

×   ×   ×

On June 24th, the 9th unit receives the order to go to Val d'Amoro to join the Monte Asolone attack. The sector assigned to the Arditi is, as always, the most heavily fortified. The Flames understand this, and their hearts pulse rapidly as they wait.

At 1550, ten minutes before the unit begins the attack, our artillery intensifies its barrage. The enemy counterattacks with rapid, wide bursts. At 1600 hours, the Arditi leap like wild animals from their foothold at quadrant 1473 and pounce at Monte Asolone.

The enemy artillery intensifies their barrage, and well-positioned machine guns fire furiously at the attackers.

In vain. Though they suffer serious losses, our soldiers keep going until they reach the first line of enemy trenches, where they launch themselves into hand-to-hand combat. It's a battle of knives and grenades. All of a sudden, from where the melee is most intense, the Arditi battle flag is raised. The Flames are electrified. The machine gun nests are taken by a frontal assault. Everything inevitably falls to their terrible onslaught. The machine gunners who don't surrender are killed on the spot, and their weapons are turned with prodigious velocity against the Austrians.

Enemy reinforcements provide continual resistance, but the Arditi, accustomed to fighting one-on-ten, keep pulling the enemy apart. Quality beats quantity. The flamethrowers clean out the caves, their sinister glow illuminating the tragic battle.

The enemy, its throat gripped by iron fists, flinches but continues to resist.

The Flames harden themselves for a supreme effort that overpowers, crushes, and destroys everything. With one last push, the crest of Monte Asolone is reached. The heroic Major Messe waves the flag of the Potenza nobility, retrieved from the blood of Ciro Scianna, a pure son of Sicily, the unit's standard bearer, who had fallen moments earlier.

After a moment's breath, the fighting continues with even greater intensity. Enemy artillery torments our captured positions and fresh machine guns unload their funeral rosaries.

The ranks of the Flames are constantly thinning. Remaining in this quadrant in such conditions is absolutely impossible. To avoid useless sacrifice, Major Messe uses all his energy to bring the Arditi back to our first line of defense, where they can regroup and defeat anyone who tries to follow.

The day following that glorious battle—that radiant poem of valor which brings the cycle of the first epic to a dignified close—the Arditi rest, covered in mud and blood, singing their songs of youthful tumult.

The recorded losses were appalling, but the will of the survivors had grown in tenacity, and shone more brilliantly.

×   ×   ×

And then came the October offensive.

It has been suggested, as part of an effort to discredit the effort of our army and devalue our great victory, that this offensive was a cakewalk, with the Austrians fleeing at the first cannon blast.

It is true that the great majority of our forces met with little resistance.

But it must be remembered that the army could only advance after the assault troops, Arditi, bikes and armored cars, had demolished the enemy front.

In his order of the day dated November 1st, 1918, General Zoppi, commander of the 1st assault division, put it thus to his Arditi:

> It was you who opened the most majestic and crucial door to today's victories. On the night of the 26th, when you crossed the Piave with eager souls, pockets full of grenades, and cases full of ammunition, when you advanced on the enemy, everything depended on you. Italy, with a trusting but anxious soul, followed in the wake of your boats, and cupped its ears to hear the first roar of your weapons.
>
> The explosion of your first grenade in the insidious gloom of the other shore was as immense, holy, and solemn as the voice of God, and it was the first principle of the new History of Italy.

To illustrate just how tremendous and bloody the fighting was on the Piave, and on the Grappa, I will cite the most revealing passages from the accounts given by unit commandants:

The Napoleonic plan for the battle that became known as Vittorio Veneto was not well received by allied high command. There were serious risks involved, and if it failed it would compromise the outcome of the war, which had been proceeding positively on the western front for the past two months.

But our high command decided to go through with it, because they knew they had the right troops for the job: the two assault divisions and various esteemed regiments of every specialty, who had made untold sacrifices for the honor and glory of Italy.

After almost two months of intense preparation and waiting, a demonstration was launched on October 23rd 1918, from the Altipiani to the Piave, and on October 26th the commandant of the 7th corps ordered his troops to cross the river (order of the day, General Caviglia, October 26th, 1918).

The journey was taken on the night of October 26th, despite the adverse weather and high water level, by the 12th army corps and the 1st assault division (order of the day, General Caviglia, November 4th, 1918), partly by wading and partly by footbridge, many of which would be carried away by the current, or destroyed by enemy artillery, such that soldiers who crossed these bridges would often end up stranded, lacking rations and ammunition.

If it hadn't corresponded to the faith of the high command, this audacious enterprise would have ended like the enemy offensive of June 1918, and our army may not have been able to stop our rapacious adversary on the Piave line. But the valiant troopers fought for two days and three nights with admirable tenacity, taking arms, ammunition, and rations from the enemy to continue fighting as they awaited help that shouldn't have been lacking.

On October 28th, the commandant of the 8th Army, deeply concerned for the fate of these troops, ordered new bridges to be constructed on the Piave to provide help and allow them to reach their defined objectives (order of the day, General Caviglia, October 28th, 1918). Thus in the night of October 28th, the 8th and 27th corps crossed the river, and the next day the 1st assault division, feeling the additional support, could continue their victorious operation, pushing onward via various paths to Vittorio Veneto and opening the way for the infantry of the 10th corps, who overwhelmed the rear of the enemy line, leading to the collapse of what was once a powerful Austrian army (order of the day, General Caviglia, November 4th, 1918).

One of the assault groups crossing the Piave on the night of October 26th had to construct the bridgehead over Moriago, Fonsigo, and Sernaglia while engaged in intense combat for three nights and two days, as mentioned in Austrian communiqués of October 28th and 29th. The tone of the Austrians was still confident, since they hoped to take advantage of the Italian troops' isolation at Moriago and Sernaglia. But the Italians were well able to resist and win, because they were animated by a spirit of sacrifice and real patriotism, rather than the mere pleasure of the hunt which was the only unifying factor in the multilingual Austrian army.

The other two groups on the Sernaglia-Villamatta line made decisive progress to the east, toppling the defenses of the Falsè di Piave, crossing the Soligo stream, attacking the high ground of Laguizza, Coltalto, and then heading north to help the 2nd assault division which, operating within the 8th corps, had to cross the Piave at Nervesa to reach Colle Guardia and Monte Cucco.

The Arditi of the 1st division admirably executed every audacious twist of the operation from the Brenta river to the sea. All of their tasks were accomplished with valor, audacity, and precision, together with the brave troops of the 8th Army, with whom they fought and won the battle of Vittorio Veneto, thus deserving, according to high command, "national recognition."

×   ×   ×

As for the Grappa, we can take the 9th unit as the model, since they received the honor of a special citation, along with the 18th and 23rd units, in Diaz's communiqué of October 26th.

Here's how the battle played out:

The Arditi are well-aware that the battle that has just begun will be the most bitter of all, because the task entrusted to the troops is to provoke the arrival of as many enemy reserves (currently bivouacked in the Feltrino) as possible.

They know this involves returning to the Asolone, and are happy to resume the match that was interrupted back in June.

At 0500 hours, the Flames reach Val Damoro and deploy on the first lines facing quadrants 1486 and 1520.

At 0800 hours, the artillery and bombers begin a barrage of destruction fire. At 0815, unit patrols vault the trenches and pass the barbed wire, and ready themselves to push further forward once the artillery begins firing further ahead.

Morale, needless to say, is extremely high. At 0828, the unit dashes like lightning. One company heads toward quadrant 1486 and the other two proceed resolutely toward quadrant 1520. Their advance is rapid. The enemy is taken by surprise, overwhelmed, devastated, captured. Nothing can stop the impetus of the Flames, who reach the ridge of Casera Stra in one mad rush. They occupy the lowest part of the Val delle Saline, attack quadrants 1471 and 1476, smash the enemy defenses and swoop down on Col della Berretta, which after fierce battle falls into our hands. The prisoners already number more than six hundred, and a good number of machine guns have been captured. The devastated enemy of Col della Berretta retreat toward Col Bonato, followed by our troops, who also reach quadrant 1127.

There is something especially momentous about this achievement. The Arditi lightning strike has dealt a serious blow to the defensive capabilities of the enemy who react desperately after the first shock.

Reinforcements come from every direction. Enemy artillery batters Col della Berretta and other positions, while machine guns hammer down from nearby quadrants. The struggle assumes tragic proportions: it's twenty against one, but the Flames won't quit. Daggers dig viciously into the bodies of those who dare to approach. Three times, the Arditi, who assume a circular formation, fight off the Austrians with a fantastic shower of grenades. But the situation is almost hopeless. The enemy, realizing that there are so few troops on the front line, continually refresh their forces, and counterattack with stubbornness and valor, but our troops maintain their resistance and cut off the enemy attack once more.

Our boldly exposed and skillfully maneuvered machine guns inflict carnage on the enemy, but reinforcements keep coming. Finally, still fighting, our troops begin to withdraw, in orderly fashion despite the violent barrage.

The last group to pull back, formed by the unit commandant, the standard-bearer officer and about twenty Arditi, suddenly finds itself cut off by an enemy unit.

Ferocious combat ensues with carbines and grenades. The Arditi need to pass at all cost, and try to break through by cutting down as many enemy soldiers as possible.

After over half an hour of tormented battle, some Arditi who had already withdrawn come in search of their major and swoop down on the enemy unit. Together with the few who remained of the trapped soldiers, they force the enemy to disarm. The withdrawal is thus a success, despite the intense barrage of enemy artillery and machine guns.

After this legendary day which cost the lives of thirteen officers and two hundred fifty troopers, Major Messe wrote the following to a friend:

"As in all the earlier battles, it was the conduct of the officers and the troops that was truly heroic."

We must also add that on this occasion the Flames had fulfilled their task in a manner higher than all praise.

×   ×   ×

On October 29th, Monte Asolone is once again the theater of bloody battle. The Arditi, who had been replaced for three days due to the attrition of the October 25th, return to battle. No one wants to stay in the Pove barracks, and provisions are rather thin.

The unit provisions officer, Lieutenant Zanfarino Maurizio from Sassari, who later died heroically on the battlefield, had been relieved of that sensitive post so that he could participate in operations.

The objectives are still the same as three days earlier. It is essential to ensure that no enemy units leave the Grappa. To achieve this, a sufficiently powerful offensive is required so that the enemy believe a mortal blow might be dealt against them on this front.

Again, the Flames spare no effort.

At 0934, the Arditi, impatient from waiting, vault the trenches, pass the barbed wire and run straight for the enemy positions. The weather is dreadful. It is cold, with an incredibly dense fog, and soft, maddening sleet covering everything. Visibility is atrocious, favoring the enemy more than us, since artillery and machine gun fire is prepared and calculated in advance.

The first trenches of the Asolone are quickly traversed, and the fight is taken as deep as possible. The machine gun nests, well protected, inflict heavy enough casualties, but the Austrians lose more. Sweeping aside all who resist, opening the way with showers of grenades, catching soldiers and machine guns in the blaze of flamethrowers, the Arditi advance.

They can barely see a thing, and our soldiers can only make themselves known by calling their major's name.

The left flank of the column pointing toward Col della Berretta—quadrant 1486 unexpectedly still in enemy hands—faces a serious threat from the enemy pouring in from Val della Salina in an effort to outflank our forces.

A large patrol is ordered to reinforce the vulnerable column at the head of the valley, where the enemy is trying to emerge. Fighting rages on for a quarter of an hour, until the enemy is once again overwhelmed and massacred.

The Flames then proceed toward Col della Berretta. Casa Spallanzani and Cason delle Fratte become centers of furious combat upon their arrival. The machine guns hammer every corner of the battlefield. The ranks of the Flames are thinning out. The standard bearer officer is gravely wounded, but the flag of the 9th never stops waving. Another hero gathers it up and carries it like some terrible wager making the fight more tragic and more glorious.

The persistent fog allows the enemy to infiltrate. Our soldiers are forced to split into ever smaller groups to counter attacks from every direction.

Courageously positioned machine guns inflict carnage on the enemy, but the holes in the ranks of the Flames are ever deeper.

The survivors are now few and far between. Almost all the officers are dead or wounded. Major Messe is injured by shrapnel from a hand grenade during a bitter struggle with a Hungarian officer, but refuses to leave the field. Held up by two Arditi, he continues to direct the action. After the major's example, everyone multiplies their forces and holds their ground in the face of an enemy twenty times more numerous. The flag of the ladies of Potenza flies high, where the melee is the most ferocious.

The officer who holds it, Lieutenant Zanfarino, is hit in the throat by a burst of machine gun fire, severing his carotid artery. Beside him, Major Messe takes the standard away and tries his best to bandage the wound, but Zanfarino won't let him: "It's useless," he manages to say. With great effort, he rises to his feet and charges at the closest enemy. With his last drop of blood, he cries his last cry: "Italy!" The Flames are now only a handful, as the enemy pushes deeper with their reinforcements. They come from every direction, from Val Cesilla, from the ruins of Col Caprile, from Valloni down to the Brenta.

The most Arditi of the Arditi still resist, counterattacking whenever the enemy gets too close, and for more than an hour they manage to contain them. In the evening, still putting up a superb fight, the few dozen remaining, including Major Messe being dragged along, begin to withdraw.

The fighting of October 29th, due to both the intensity of combat and the dire weather conditions, was without doubt one of the most atrocious battles fought by the unit, and the glorious page written by the black Flames that day was certainly among the most resplendent.

×   ×   ×

November 2nd, a day for all the dead. The 10th unit, replenished with fresh elements, is ordered to pursue the enemy. On horseback, they take the road from the Brenta leading to Borgo via Cimson and Tezze.

The black Flames have wings on their feet. They overwhelm rearguard fortifications, capture cannons, machine guns, prisoners, and supply carts.

The enemy aren't given a minute's rest. The moment they try to resist, the Flames are upon them, cutting them off. Every soldier carries the vivid memory of those distant days of October 1917, and wants to inflict the same agony on the enemy who had inflicted it on us.

Along the Val Brenta the Arditi can finally see the results of their efforts.

In the crazed clash that ensues, many of the Italian prisoners, used for rear-line duties by the enemy, are liberated. They relate their experiences and our hearts fill with desire for revenge.

The pursuit accelerates as it reaches Solva. None of those barbarians can escape. The captured prisoners number in the thousands.

Every now and then, the Arditi encounter a machine gun nest which they courageously defeat by—as always—forcing them to give up with a shower of grenades. Our loot piles higher, and the pursuit gets faster and faster.

A group of our bravest soldiers, on horses taken from the enemy, charges at a gallop and persuades a retreating unit to surrender.

The Flames, who have been marching for almost two days, never ask for rest; they stop only when they reach Borgo, at 1500 hours on November 4th.

×   ×   ×

In the *Giornale d'Italia,* high command recently published casualty statistics for the last two battles, divided by specialty.

Here we learn that "the highest percentage of sacrifice came from the assault units." As Achille Benedetti writes, "the magnificent, impetuous and—contrary to the superficial beliefs of the public—disciplined Arditi lost 20 percent of their forces on the battlefield," while infantry lost 16 percent, bombers lost 7, bersaglieri lost 6, and the autonomous machine gun companies lost 5 percent.

Types of Arditi

Because they embody the characteristics that are most alive in the Italian temperament, the Arditi corps was composed of a wide range of often contradictory types.

There was the apostle possessed by a superior idealism, which found in the assault unit the most heroic and complete means by which to achieve those ideals. And there was the dilettante of the dagger, who saw his persecuted and slandered "companion in adventure" bestowed the dignity of a national weapon.

There was the sentimental idealist who saw in these battalions of death a renewed Garibaldianism. And there was the daredevil with abundant energy, who had to escape the monotonous gray of the infantry regiments.

There were—let's be honest—veterans of the country's prisons, who asked the country for a way to rehabilitate themselves. But there was also the most pure, wise, and brilliant Italian who never deviated for an instant from his divine mission as the leading patrolman of every march, ideal or real.

All were driven by one desire: killing as many Austrians as possible. All were inspired by the same religion: victory. All were armed with the same magnificent weapon: courage.

Courage was the mark of distinction uniting in brotherhood the pale dreamer and the former knife-wielding criminal, the haughty aristocrat and the futurist, the gymnast and the idealist.

×   ×   ×

I have seen so many, in the atmosphere of heroism, pounce with a great shout, drop with great poise, powerful figures worthy of a diabolical chisel . . . But how few names I remember!

Some, nevertheless, survive in my memory.

Who hasn't heard of Ciro Scianna? Sicilian, soul and blood of fire, simple soldier, standard bearer, who stirred the company to attack, running and waving the banner in the most fiery battle zones, shouting, roaring imperious commands. A captivating example of beauty and faith. Mowed down by a machine gun, he called over his major (the heroic Messe), handed him the banner, asked to see it once more, splashed it with his blood and died in the conquered trench crying *"viva l'Italia!"*

The little urchin Padovani, sweet and proud, illiterate Neapolitan, my messenger on Solarolo, who spent the whole night bringing reports, Austrian machine guns and prisoners from quadrant 1671, where five of us were holding the position, to battalion command, under incessant suppressive fire preventing the arrival of any reinforcements.

Corporal Major Lindo Andreani, who with only two soldiers on Col Moschin, faced a group of twenty-six Austrians led by an officer, and forced them to surrender.

Second Lieutenant Ponzio di San Sebastiano, adjutant of my unit, who disobeyed the commandant's order not to participate in the fighting, and charged with the first attack wave. He was wounded in both legs as a dear companion died next to him. He was carried away crying for his friend, and his inability to stay on the battlefield. Later he would send a note to the commandant apologizing for his disobedience and declaring his readiness to face disciplinary action. A boy of the 1900s!

Ottone Rosai, a magnificent Florentine, already fearless before the war, a bronze-fisted colossus who scoffed at the Austrians. On the Bainsizza, with four comrades to whom he had cried "whoever doesn't join me is a coward" he captured a machine gun and thirty-two marksmen, and returned to the front of the platoon of prisoners singing "Lassatece passà, semo romani . . ."[72]

The *ardito* Viviani, alone, crawled to an active Austrian machine gun, frightened off the crew with a hand grenade, and quickly turned the gun on the enemy.[73]

Sergeant Antonio Graceffa, on Fagheron, with just two soldiers, managed to rout a patrol of Austrian "arditi," trap them in a cave, and persuade them to surrender with a few grenades lobbed at the entrance.

Lieutenant Feletti, a Venetian from Piave, charged at an Austrian machine gun and took his shot. Surrounded, he didn't give an inch, wrought carnage among the Austrians until, overwhelmed, he died near his home, which he'd defended ferociously to the last.

The *ardito* Materno Bonazzo, wounded, fought with redoubled ardor and dragged himself to an enemy squadron, attacking and killing with all his strength until he died crying "viva l'Italia!" through a torrent of blood.

The *ardito* Paolo Mannuzzi, seeing that a great blockade of machine guns was blocking the path of his unit in Roggia dei Mulini, charged alone at the enemy line with his flamethrower and destroyed or captured all the guns, leading to an intense melee with a large group of Hungarians, who he managed to take prisoner.

The *ardito* Felice Miglio, on his own and with no orders, having spotted an enemy machine gun that was threading through his company, hurled himself at the weapon, stabbed the gunners to death, and cleared the way for the victory of his comrades.

The field adjutant Tommaso Manzi, his chest torn open by shrapnel, responded to his captain's demand that he be transported to the medical station: "The Arditi of Italy die facing the

---

[72] "Let us pass, we are Romans" in Roman dialect.

[73] Throughout this section, the soldiers are repeatedly described with the adjective *ardito*. Ardito is always capitalized when referring to a member of the Arditi.

enemy!"

Lieutenant Trebbiani, tasked with a daring surprise attack with his company, boldly pushed into enemy lines. Nothing more was heard of him. A few days later, after the Austrians withdrew from Zenson, his body was found about three hundred meters ahead of the rest of our dead. Numerous enemy cadavers surrounded him. He and one of his soldiers (Bisesti) lay in a final fraternal embrace.

The *ardito* Nicola De Lucia, a young flamethrower carrier, born in 1899. During combat he realizes that his weapon, wet from the rain, has stopped working. It looks like he'll have to give up on a crucial assault. But he doesn't give up. His commander had ordered him to set things on fire, so he'll set things on fire, whatever the cost. Through the curtain of death, he rushes to where a small flame still burns, touches it with the end of his weapon, and tests it. It works. He returns to battle, plunges into the enemy line, welcomed by a barrage of bombs, overcomes the agony of shrapnel buried in his flesh, charges at a machine gun nest hidden in a house, attacks with his diabolical fire, and forces the enemy to surrender.

The *ardito* Migliovacca, wounded first in one leg, then in the other, looked disdainfully at his blood, in which he insisted on washing his hands, and continued to give orders while ignoring his commander, who urged him, revolver in hand, to seek medical attention. "I need to take a walk," he shouted. Returning with two enemy machine guns, he fell in front of the commander with a thigh torn apart by shrapnel, and said with a smile, "this time the walk went badly."

I could go on forever.

We Thugs

Because our masculine temperament has never had any tolerance for arrogance, deceit, scams, and foolish prohibitions; because some of us, when faced with some thieving swindler hiding behind the law, have resolved the matter with two or three decisive slaps; because, when everyone else remained neutral, we dared to intervene with the energy that distinguishes us: today, we have the reputation of being "thugs," so much so that this name and ours have become synonymous.

If I said that I am deeply saddened and offended by this slander, I would be shamelessly lying. Considering the source of the insult, it can simply be spat upon and given the following response:

"Better thugs than cowards and wimps!"

Indeed, the accusation originates solely from people in those two categories. Unfortunately, it is then repeated and spread in good faith by careless citizens who are too busy to know any better. But ignorance, in some cases, is as serious a fault as bad faith. Why parrot what one hears without the means to verify?

Our thuggery, let it be known, gentlemen of Italy, has never been anything other than an excess of generosity. It has always struck out at injustice, arrogance, fraud, and betrayal. It has always fought for the weak against the strong. It has always defended noble causes and beings who are persecuted. The women and children know this. Ask them in the little villages of Veneto where our battalions were stationed. They will tell you how much sympathy, how much harmony, how much mutual love there was. They will tell you how much polenta they offered us, seasoned with their sweetest smiles, and how many evenings we spent in their hospitable homes, dancing and singing with genuine joy.

I once asked a forthright peasant woman from Bassano:

"Do you like the Arditi, miss?"

With admiration in her eyes, she replied, "Of course, sir. They are all handsome and good, and then they go off to die singing, poor lads!

Don't talk to me about looted chicken coops, decimated trees, devastated hearths. These are things that happen in war, and the Arditi have never had a monopoly on them. How many cavalrymen and drivers can be accused of the same, if not worse?

Thugs, because one of us took out his knife at the wrong time and place? He would have done it even if he wasn't an Ardito. Can any of you tell us that he wasn't provoked?

Thugs, because we sometimes rebelled against the Carabinieri? This one has a humorous origin. Listen. One day, a truck of Arditi was speeding toward the front lines. Seeing some Carabinieri in the distance, the Arditi decided that two of them would aim their rifles at the Carabinieri as they passed, while the other two, unseen, would fire into the air. The prank worked so well that the Carabinieri rolled to the ground convinced they were wounded. Eventually, assisted by their companions and examining themselves, they realized they were unharmed. The Arditi in the truck laughed uncontrollably.

From that moment on, the Carabinieri and the Arditi were antagonists, and there was persecution and reprisal on both sides. But do you know how many infantrymen, mistreated and humiliated by the overbearing "big shots," have thanked us? They, poor devils, could only ever respond with some innocent mockery; they saw us as avengers and considered us almost like their older brothers.

In any case, this conflict with the Carabinieri, which certainly didn't benefit Italy, gradually faded away. Later, in Dalmatia, some Arditi were even seen patrolling with the Carabinieri to clear out the Yugoslav swine.

The Ardito, in any circumstance, for any struggle, for any service where there is daring to be done, is sought like a rare commodity or precious element. When there is need for him, everyone flatters him, caresses him, extols him. His presence is a source of comfort and joy. He knows how to bring the warmth of his courage and the optimism of his broad, strong smile into the most cold and mournful environments, into the hearts of those who are the most timid and uncertain.

He has a gift for making what he touches strong and healthy, and making generous those who are not. One day last summer, an Ardito came to Rome on furlough. He rushed home to find his mother in tears because the landlord, who was owed several months' rent, had handed her an eviction notice. The Ardito went to the landlord. He was certainly tough enough to make threats, but no. The Ardito takes out his furlough, reads it to the gruff landlord, and says:

"Do you have the heart to throw the mother of an Ardito on the street?"

Tears came to the landlord's eyes, and the Ardito's mother stayed in her home.

Definition

From *boldness* and *ardor*, the *Ardito* was born.

Some have tried to define him as a romantic of the new Italy. Others have seen in him the Garibaldian spirit in a different uniform. Others see elements of Gasconism, etc.

I will also attempt a definition. One that summarizes the impressions I have scattered through these pages.

I see in the Arditi the triumph of a very modern and very Italian youth, untouched by skepticism and corrosive experience. The explosion of a race with powerful instincts: powerful muscles wrapped in throbbing nerves, unscrupulous and sharp intelligence, overflowing hearts and veins, the soundest guts, an inexhaustible desire to march at the front: wherever the destination, whatever danger awaits.

The Ardito is agile, impetuous, and hates all that is slow, tired, discouraged, heavy.

And since these are also the characteristics of the futurist, I believe I am not wrong in defining the Ardito as "the futurist of war," just as the futurist can be defined as "the Ardito of artistic and political battles."

I know that this definition will irritate many people. I don't know what to tell you. The fact is that almost all the futurists have fought among the Arditi, and countless Arditi have joined the Futurist Political Party.

ENJOYED THIS BOOK?

TO READ MORE, VISIT US AT

ANTELOPEHILLPUBLISHING.COM

www.ingramcontent.com/pod-product-compliance
Lightning Source LLC
Chambersburg PA
CBHW030300130626
46549CB00002B/617